MW00817494

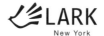

LARK
New York

An Imprint of Sterling Publishing Co., Inc.
1166 Avenue of the Americas
New York, NY 10036

ISBN 978-1-4549-2135-6

Distributed in Canada by Sterling Publishing Co., Inc.
c/o Canadian Manda Group, 664 Annette Street
Toronto, Ontario, Canada M6S 2C8
Distributed in the United Kingdom by GMC Distribution Services
Castle Place, 166 High Street, Lewes, East Sussex, England BN7 1XU

For information about custom editions, special sales, and
premium and corporate purchases, please contact Sterling Special Sales
at 800-805-5489 or specialsales@sterlingpublishing.com.

Manufactured in Canada

10   9

www.sterlingpublishing.com
www.larkcrafts.com

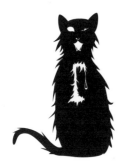

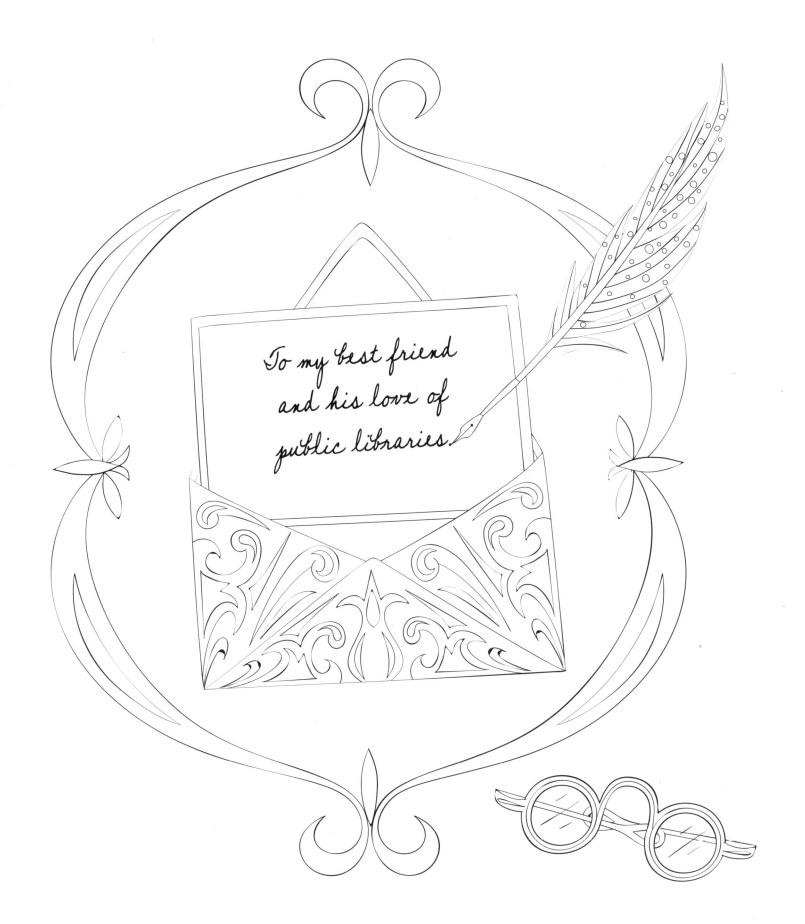

Introduction

GENERALLY, LOVE STORIES tend to go one of two ways: They have a happy ending, or they have a sad ending. It's safe to say Poe favored the latter. His stories were dark and often macabre. They were filled with grief, loss, and longing. But though they were undoubtedly morose and melancholy, to me they were love stories nonetheless.

When it came to illustrating Poe's stories, it was important to me to capture this duality of sadness and beauty. My goal was to show not just the darkness that consumed the characters and their worlds but also the intricate beauty of what they longed for—the love they once had that was now hopelessly lost. Love is a beautiful thing, but in Poe's world, longing for it is painful and dark. To put it another way, you can't know the pain of longing without having first known the beauty of love.

Poe's stories were also filled with rich and imaginative symbolism. There were men trapped beneath the shadows of ravens, bleeding hearts pulsing beneath the floorboards, a man's grief for his lost wife physically manifested by a barren and dying landscape. Combining pretty and decorative details with the extremely symbolic and morose themes of Poe's work was a unique and exciting opportunity that I hope has led to illustrations that are just as unique and exciting to color.

Poe is also considered the first author of the detective story, and so I felt it was important to include The Dupin Tales amongst this collection as well. While they're not nearly as melancholy or bloody as some of his other works, they have a powerful air of mystery and intrigue that make them just as fun to read as they were to draw.

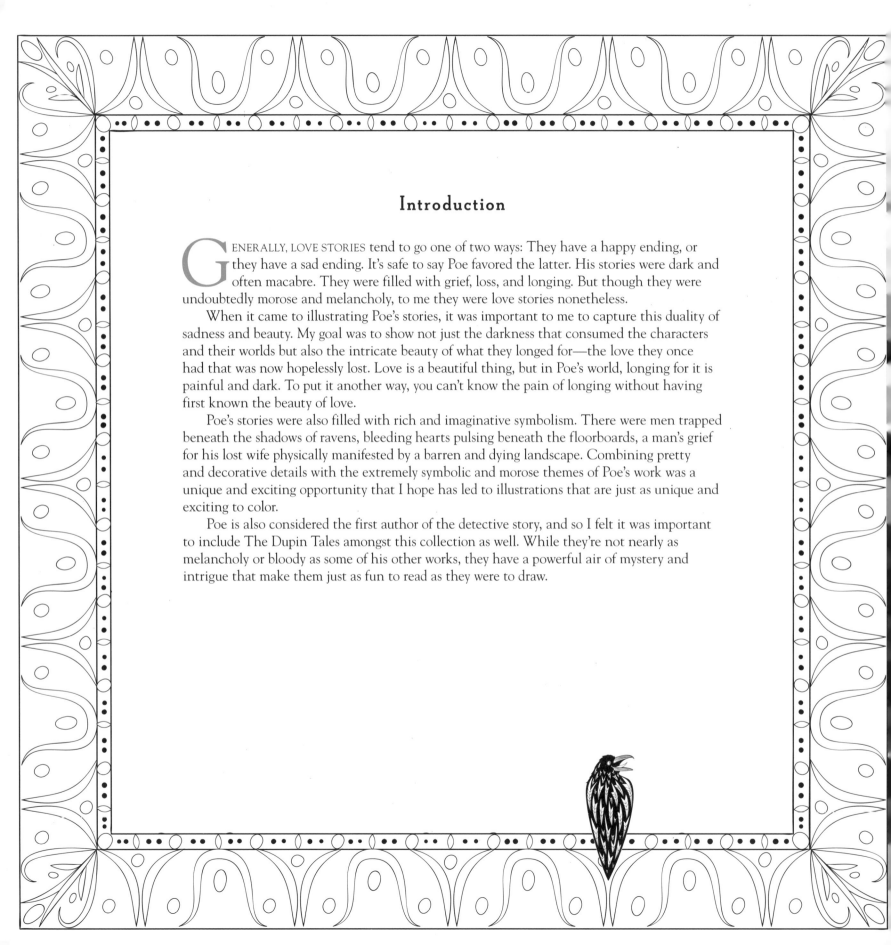

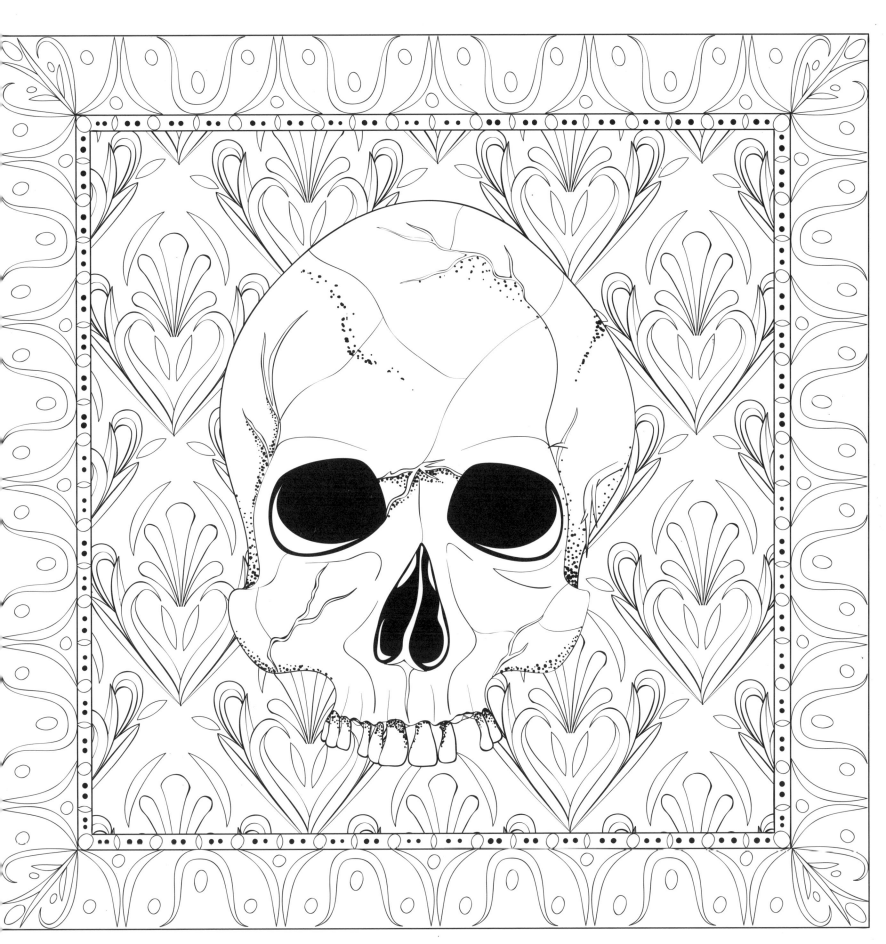

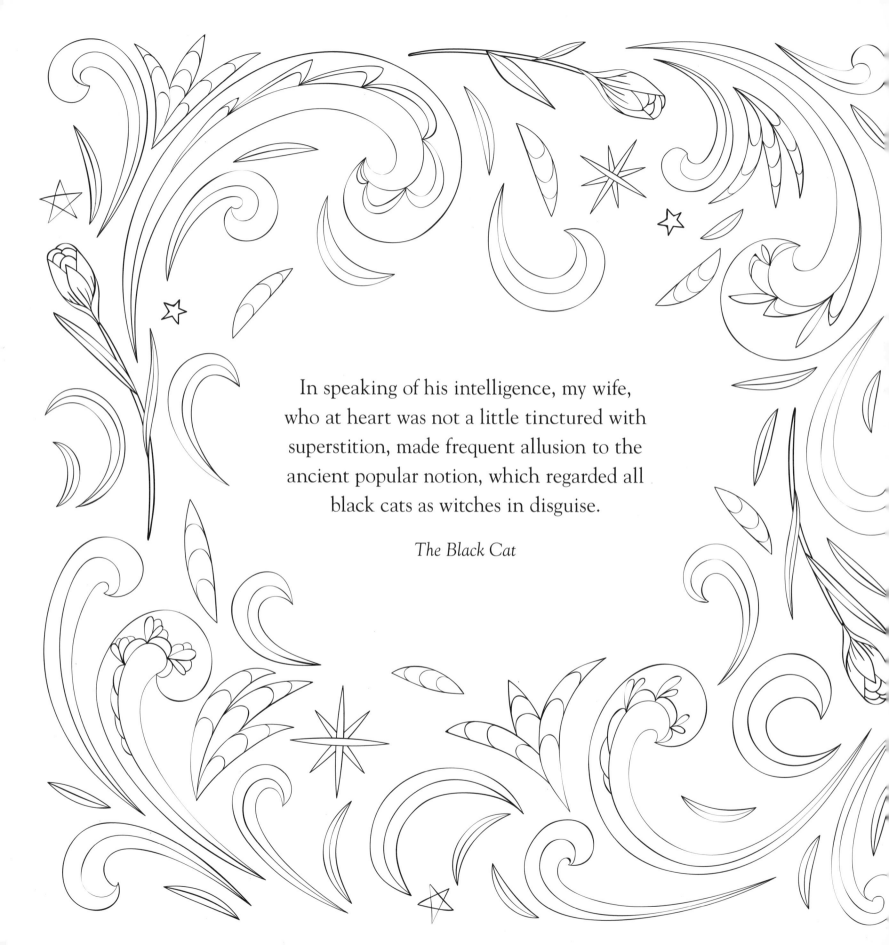

In speaking of his intelligence, my wife, who at heart was not a little tinctured with superstition, made frequent allusion to the ancient popular notion, which regarded all black cats as witches in disguise.

The Black Cat

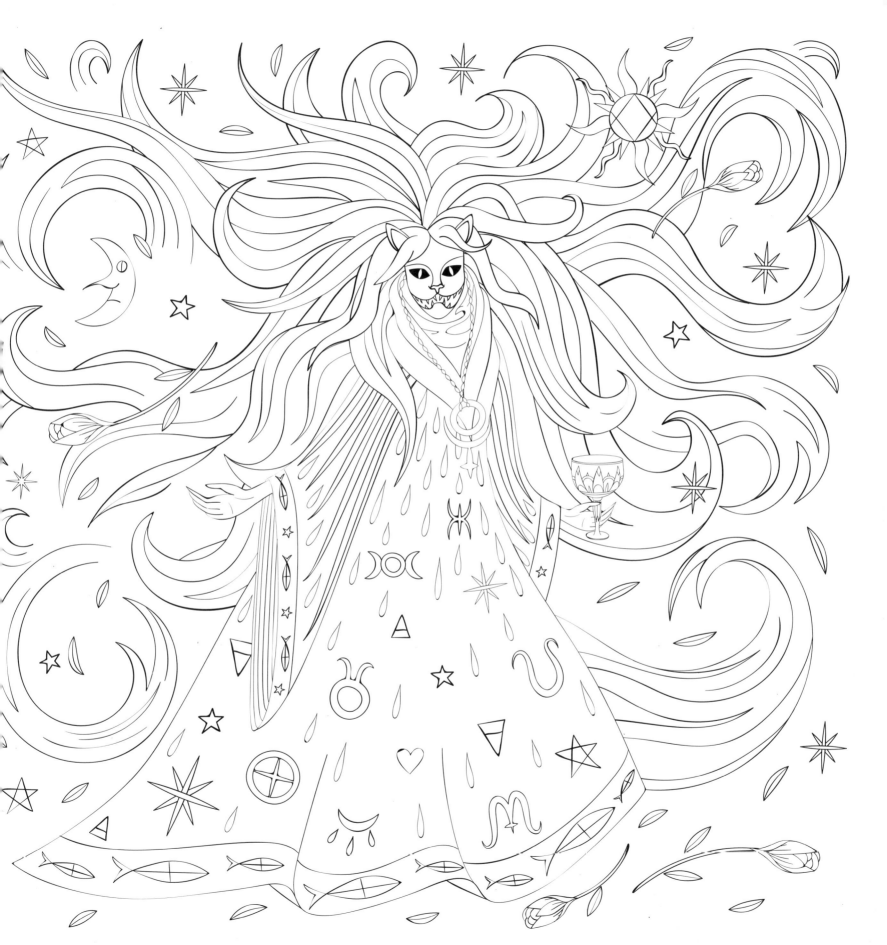

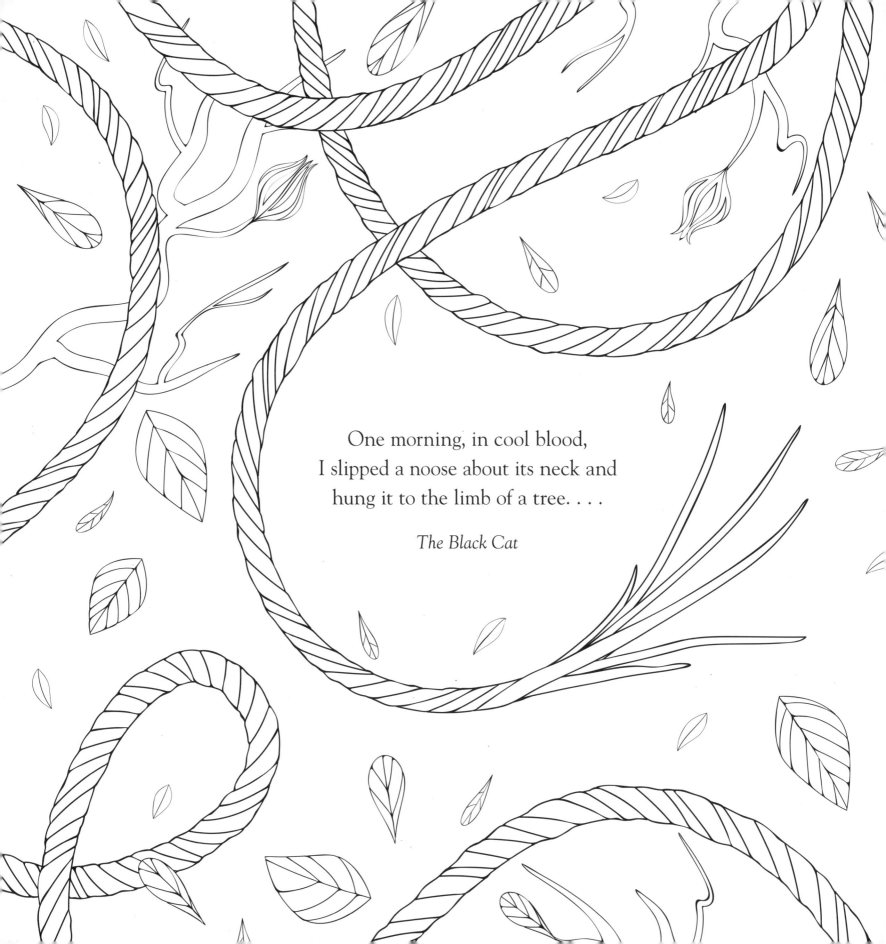

One morning, in cool blood,
I slipped a noose about its neck and
hung it to the limb of a tree. . . .

The Black Cat

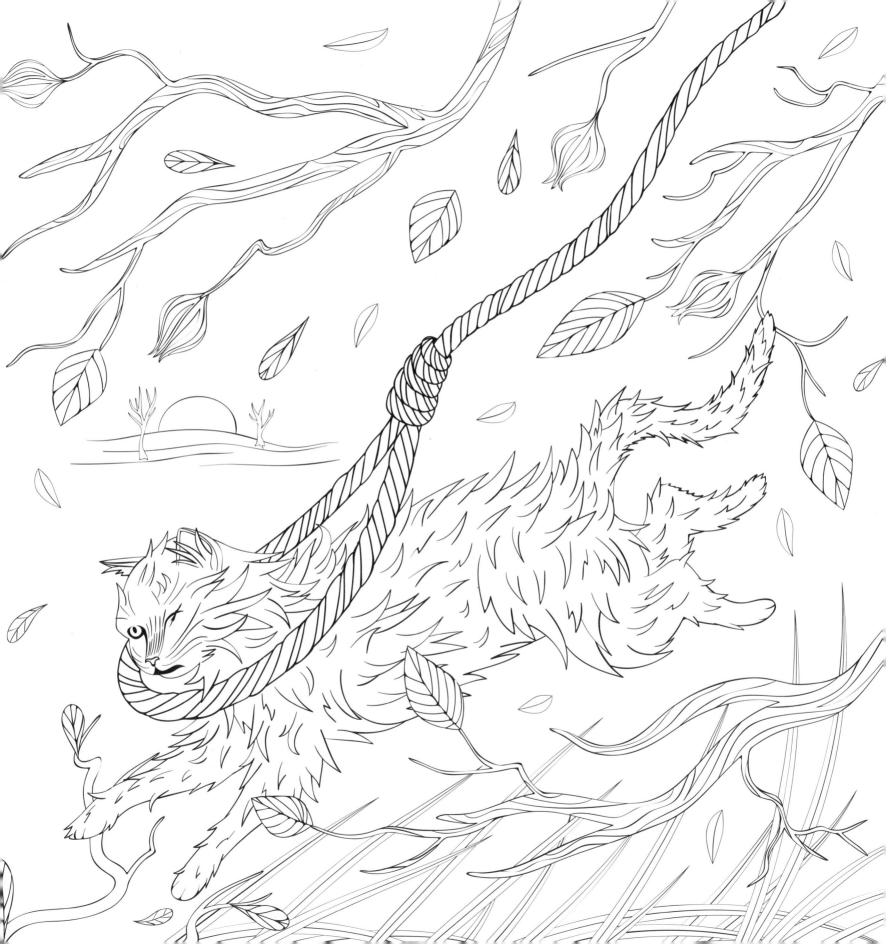

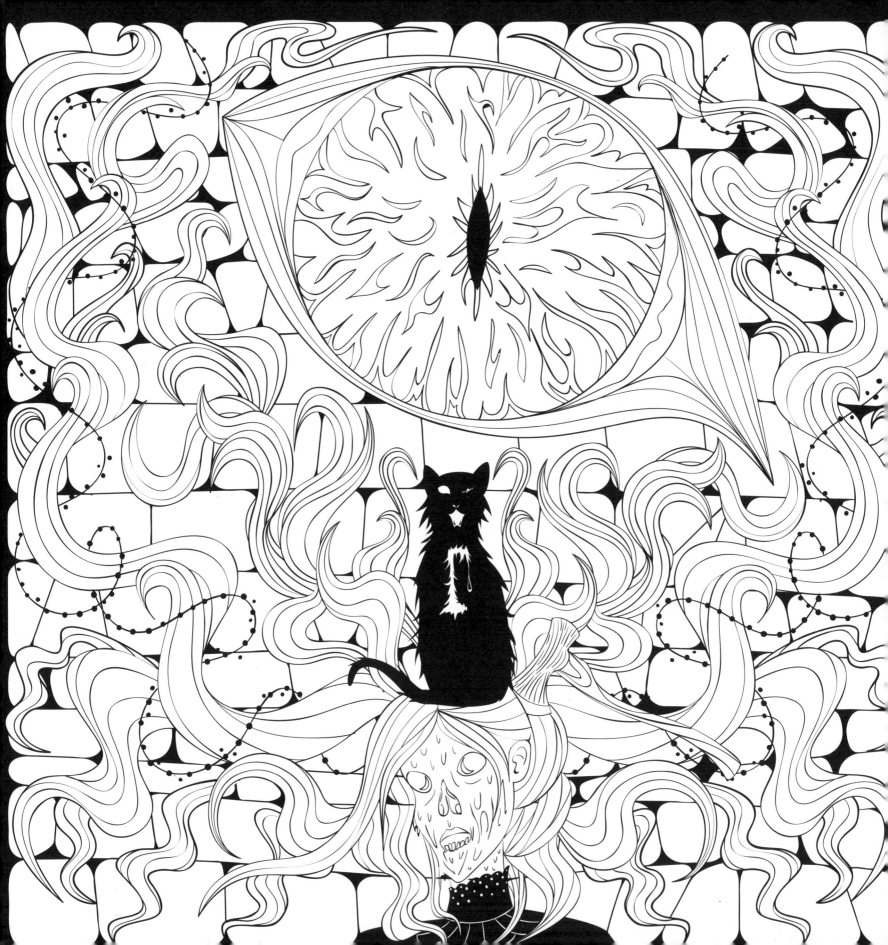

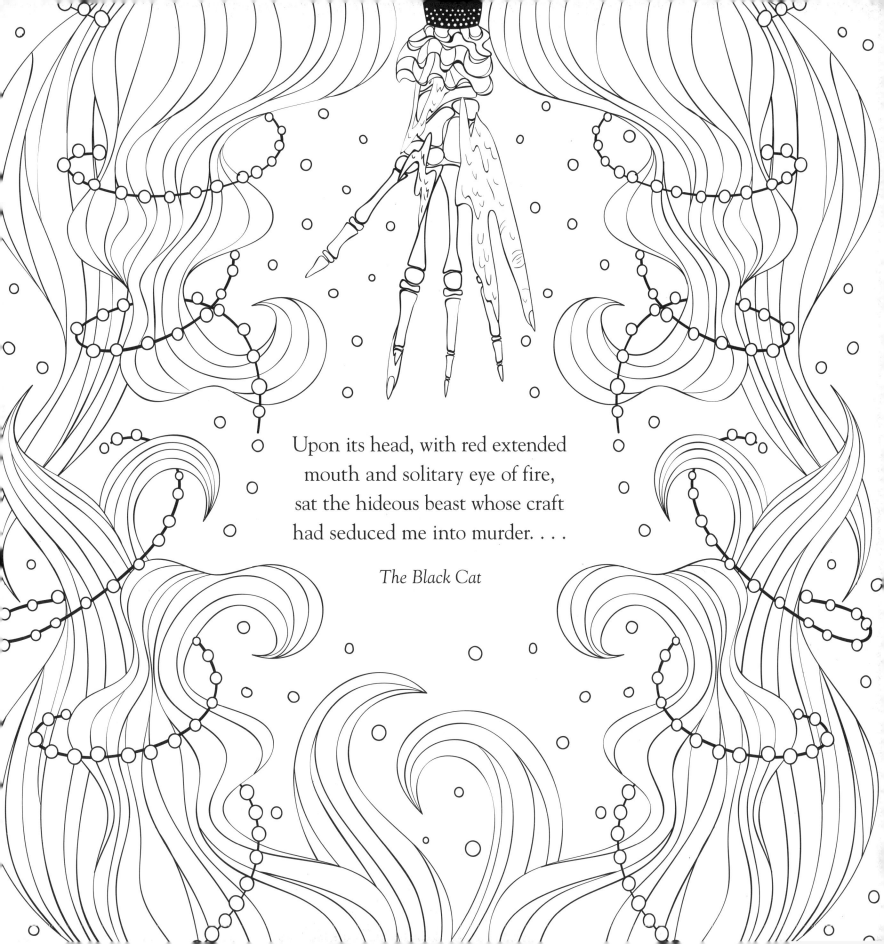

Upon its head, with red extended
mouth and solitary eye of fire,
sat the hideous beast whose craft
had seduced me into murder. . . .

The Black Cat

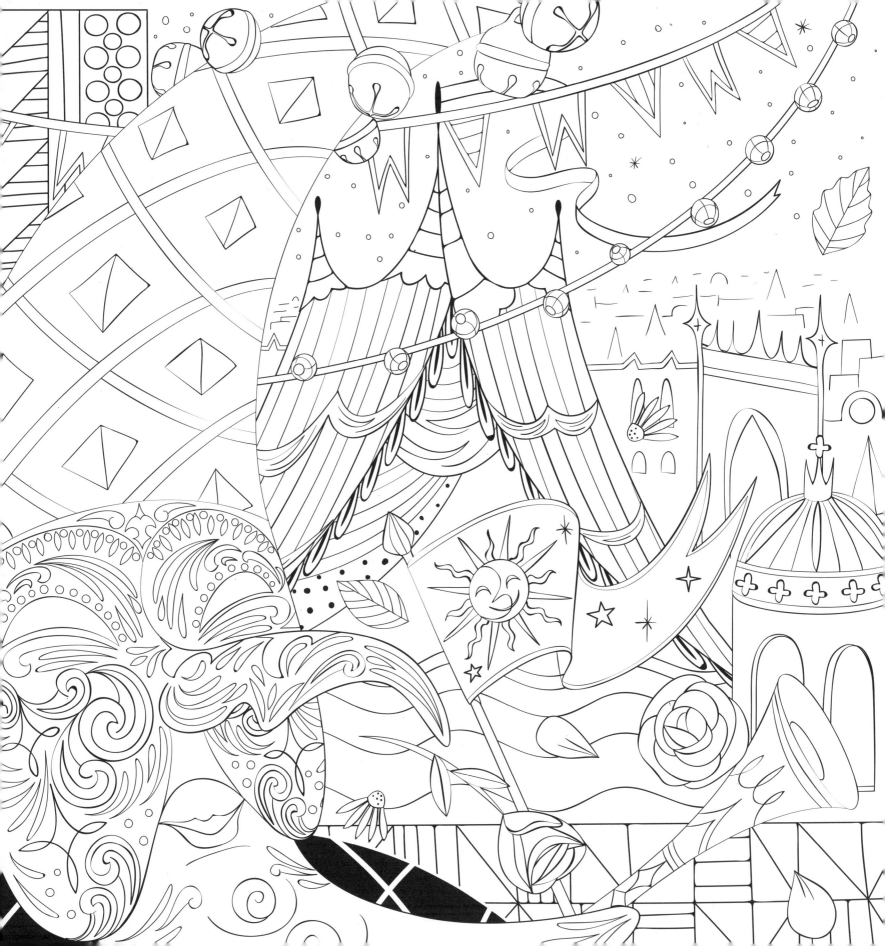

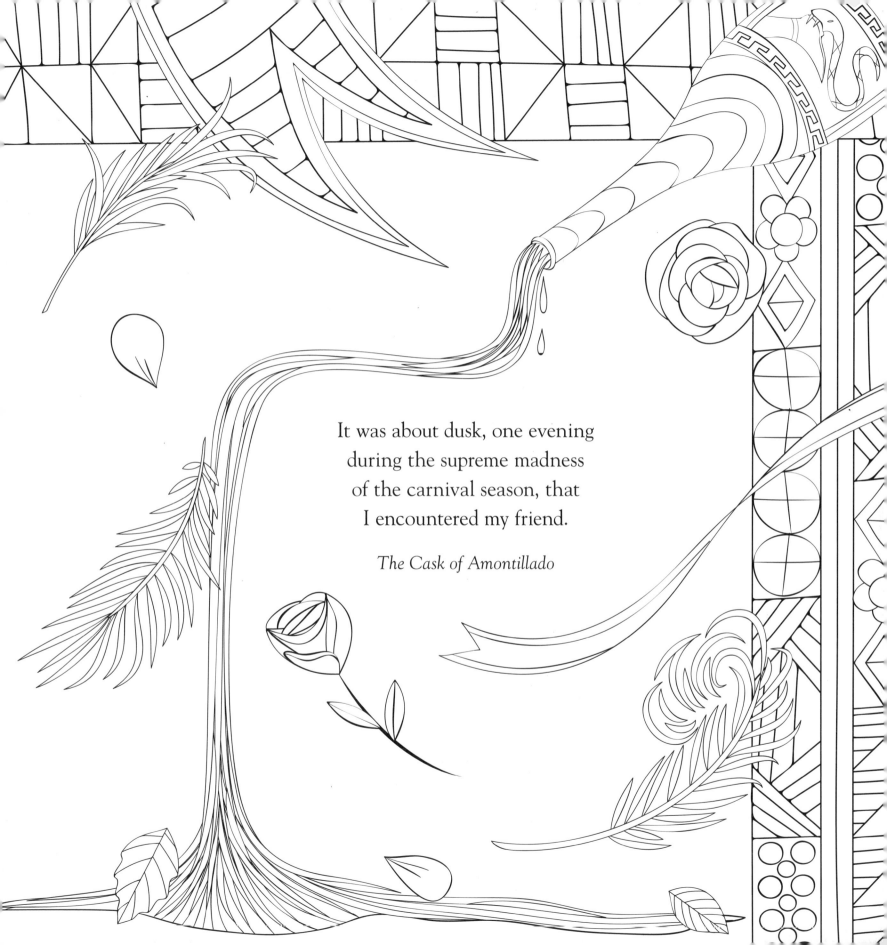

It was about dusk, one evening
during the supreme madness
of the carnival season, that
I encountered my friend.

The Cask of Amontillado

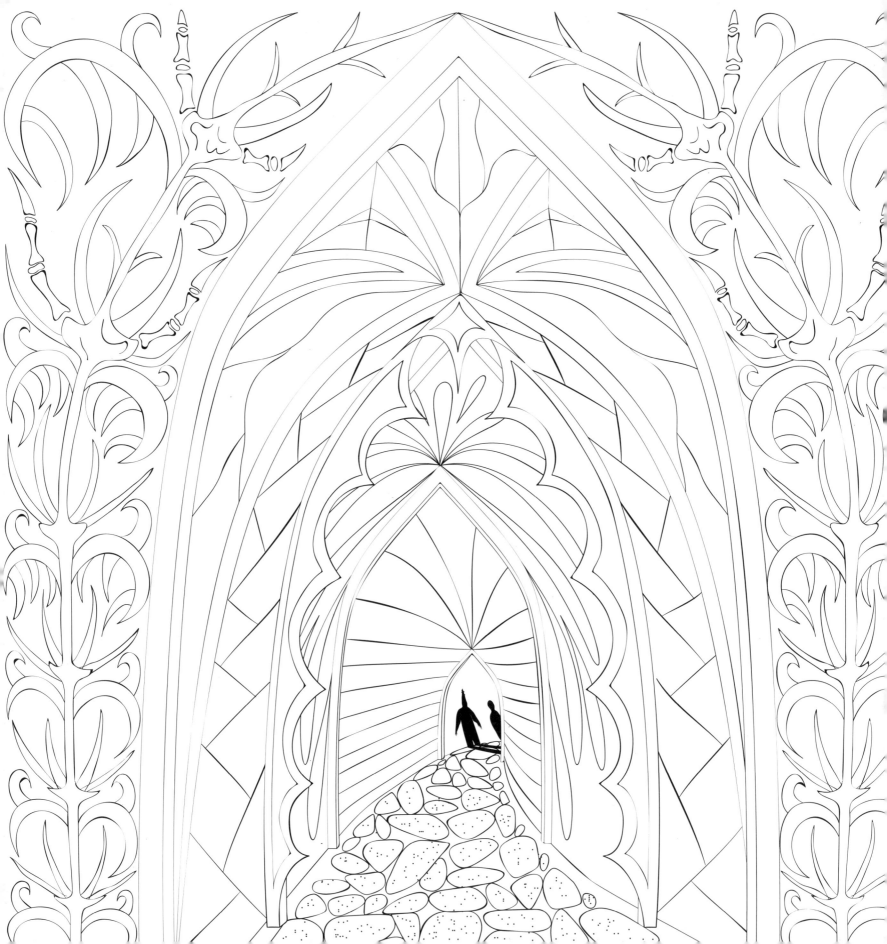

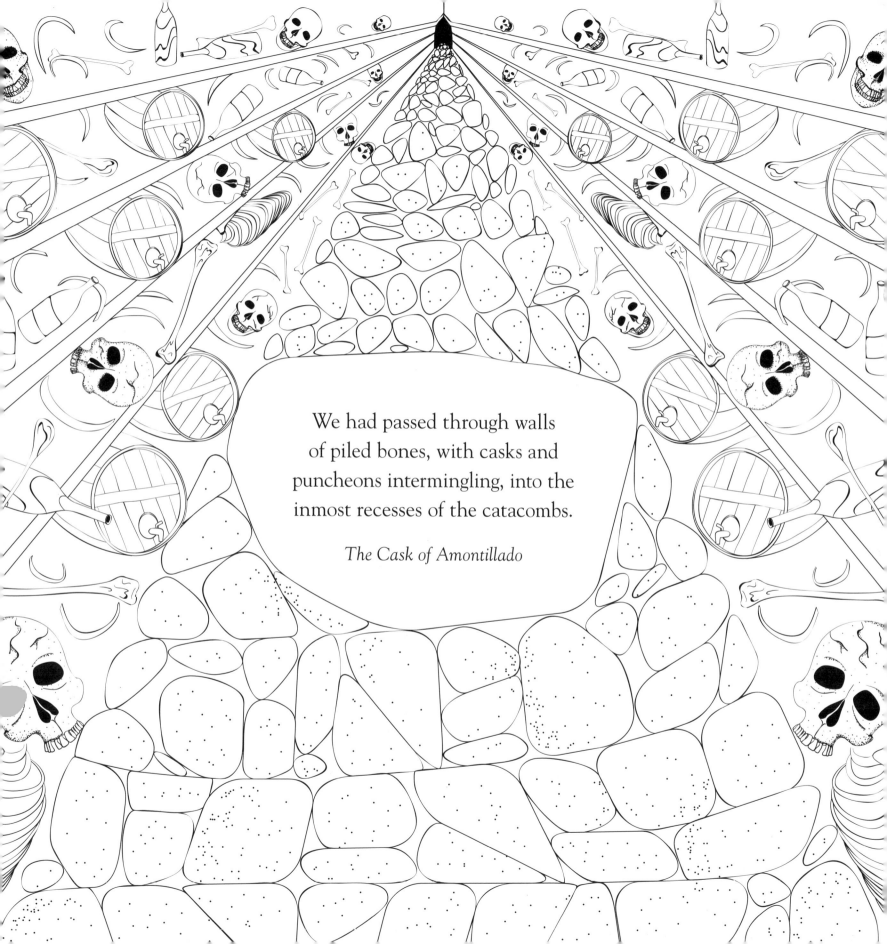

We had passed through walls of piled bones, with casks and puncheons intermingling, into the inmost recesses of the catacombs.

The Cask of Amontillado

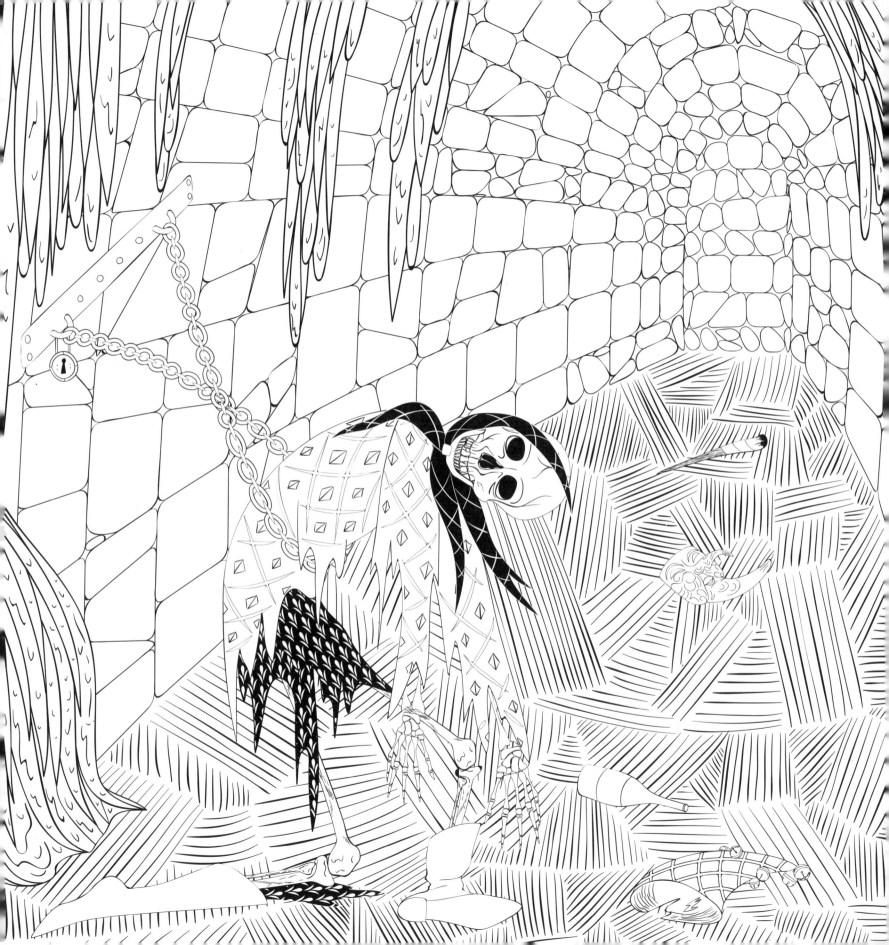

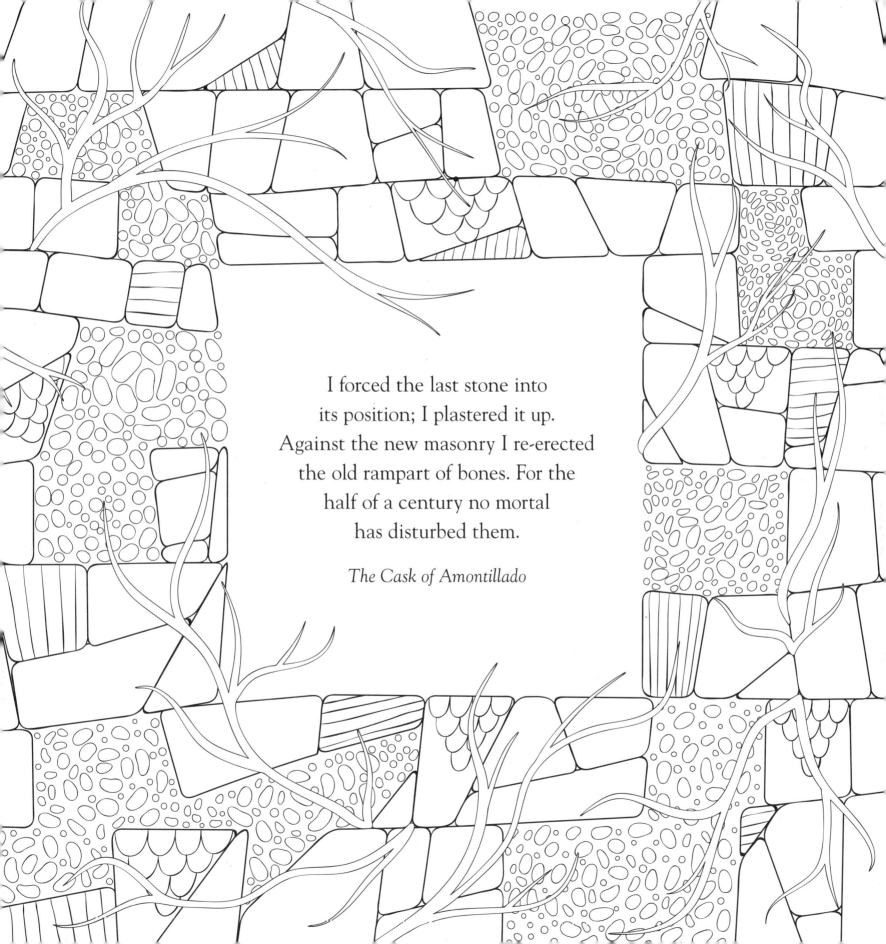

I forced the last stone into
its position; I plastered it up.
Against the new masonry I re-erected
the old rampart of bones. For the
half of a century no mortal
has disturbed them.

The Cask of Amontillado

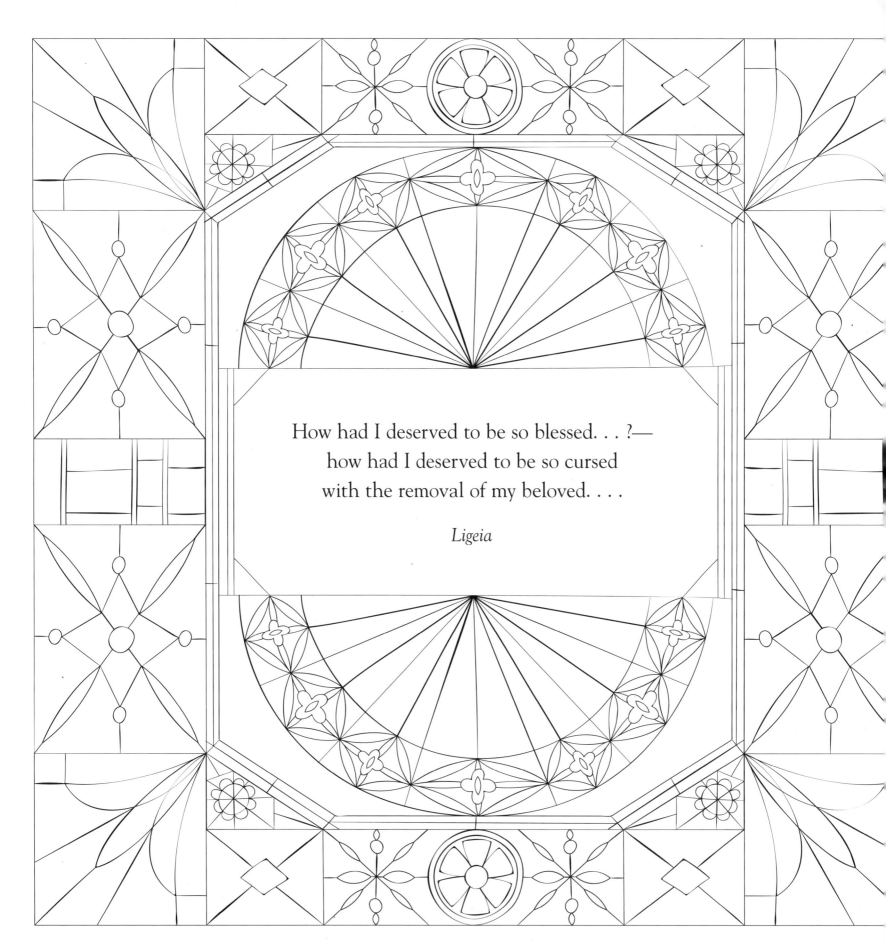

How had I deserved to be so blessed. . . ?—
how had I deserved to be so cursed
with the removal of my beloved. . . .

Ligeia

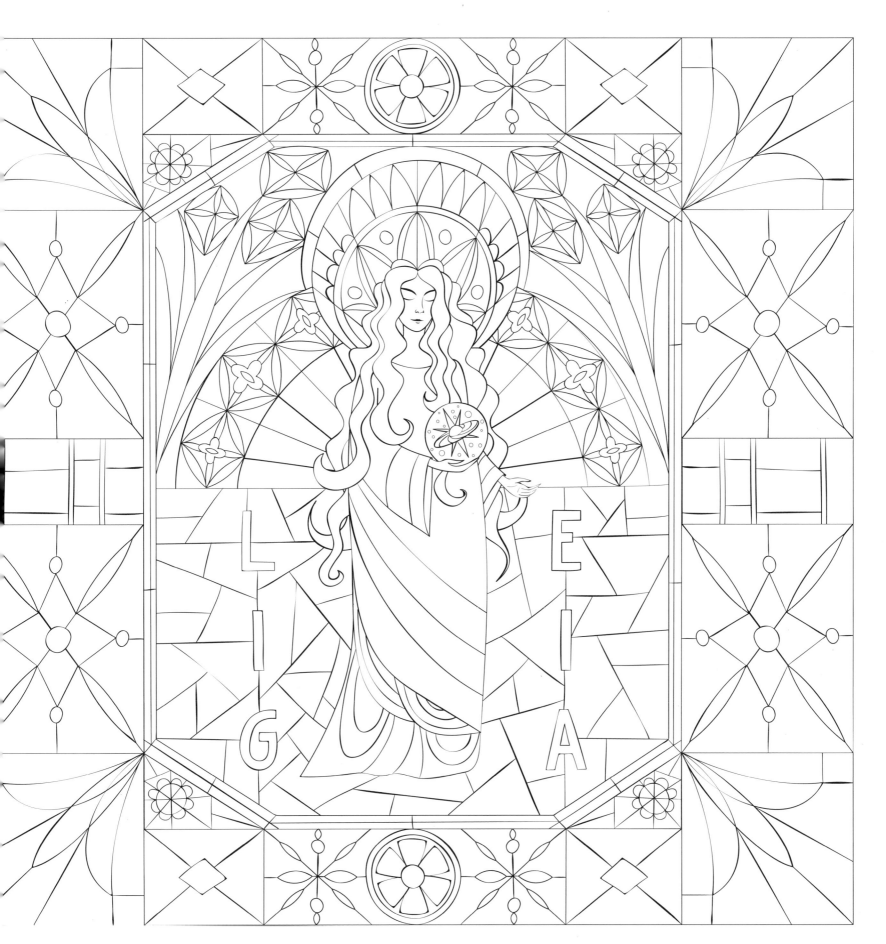

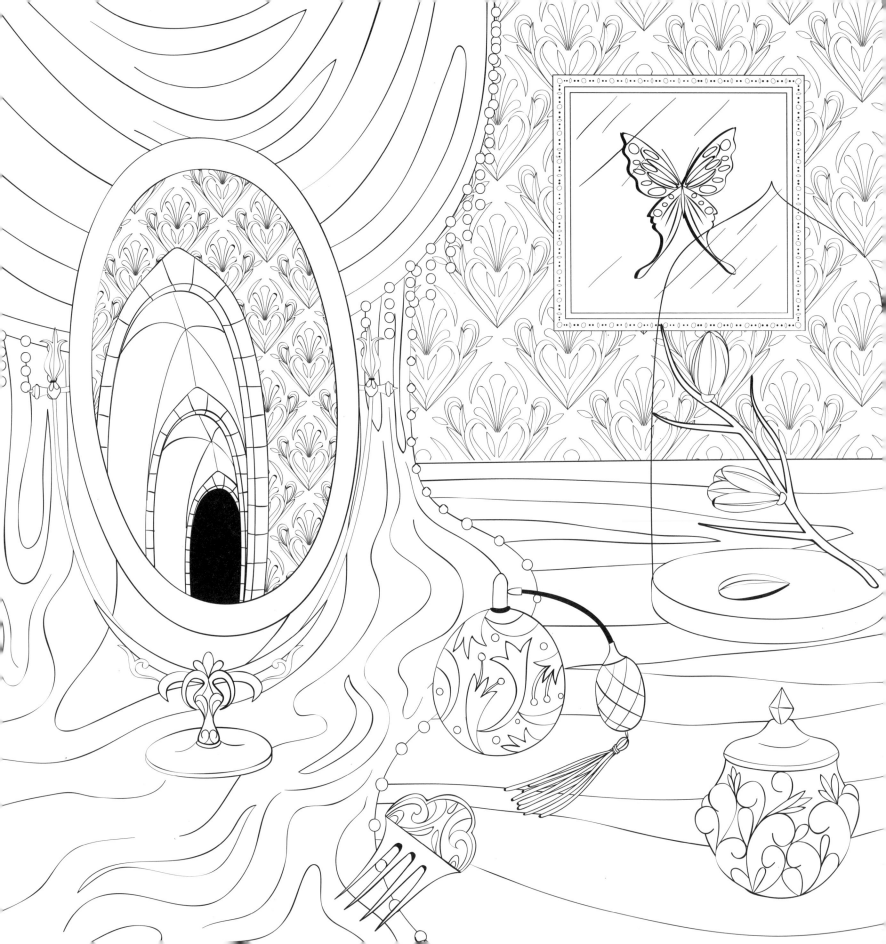

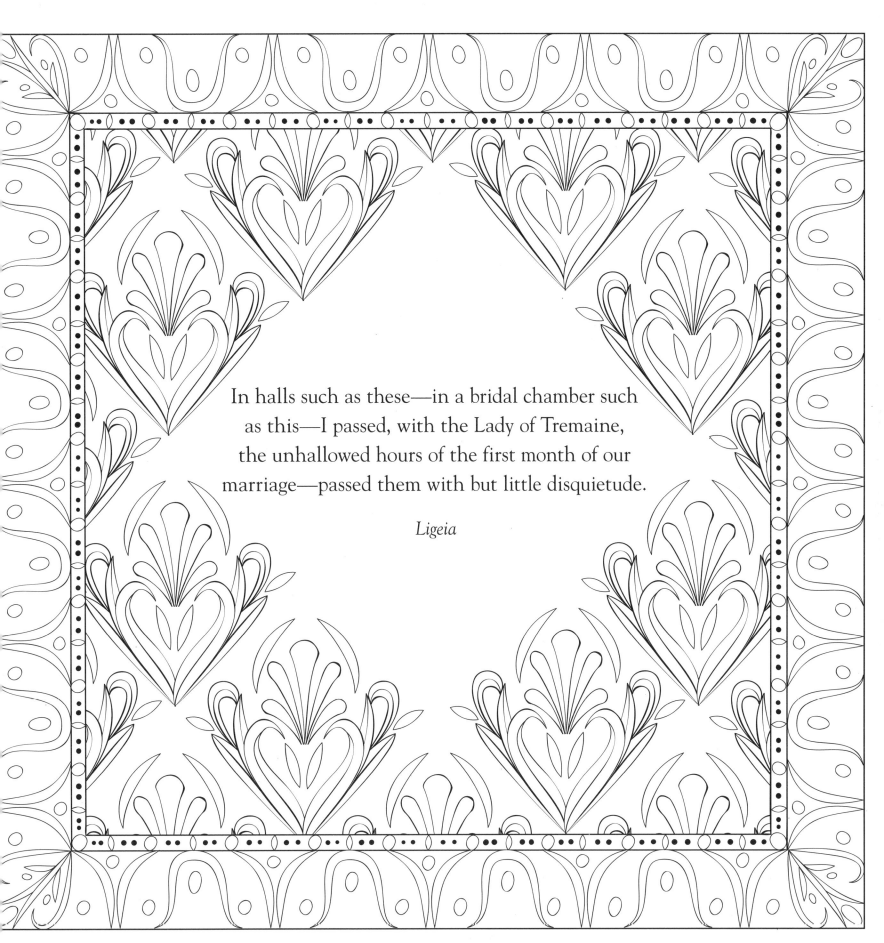

In halls such as these—in a bridal chamber such as this—I passed, with the Lady of Tremaine, the unhallowed hours of the first month of our marriage—passed them with but little disquietude.

Ligeia

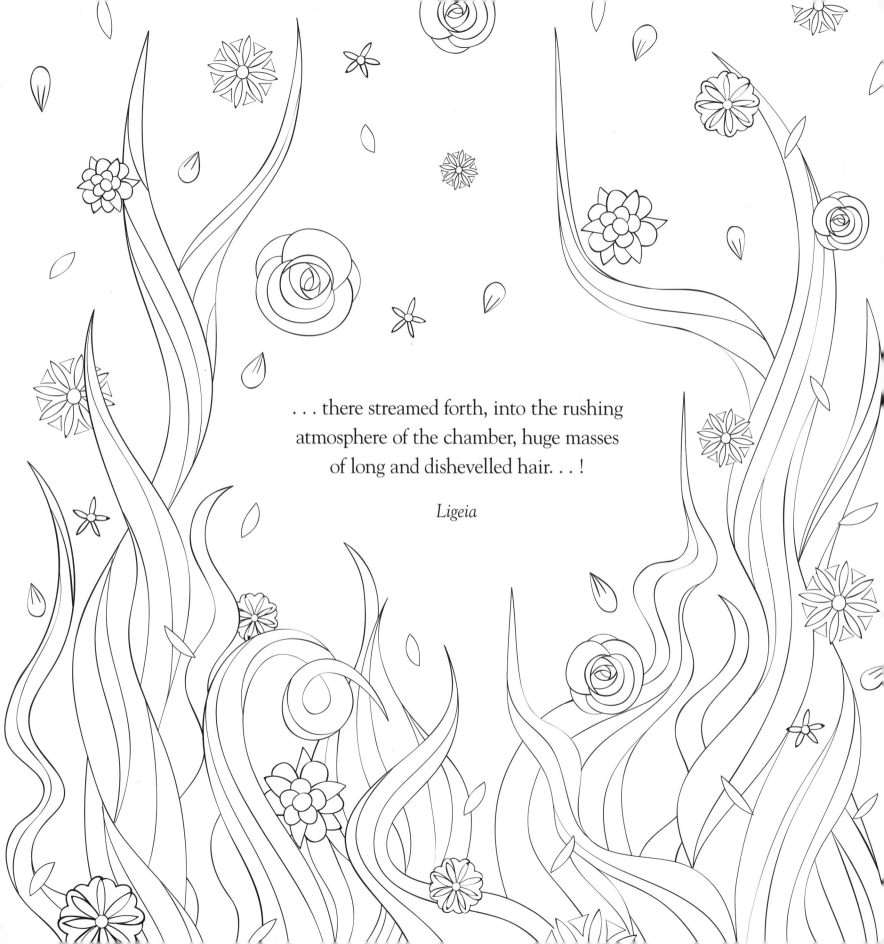

. . . there streamed forth, into the rushing
atmosphere of the chamber, huge masses
of long and dishevelled hair. . . !

Ligeia

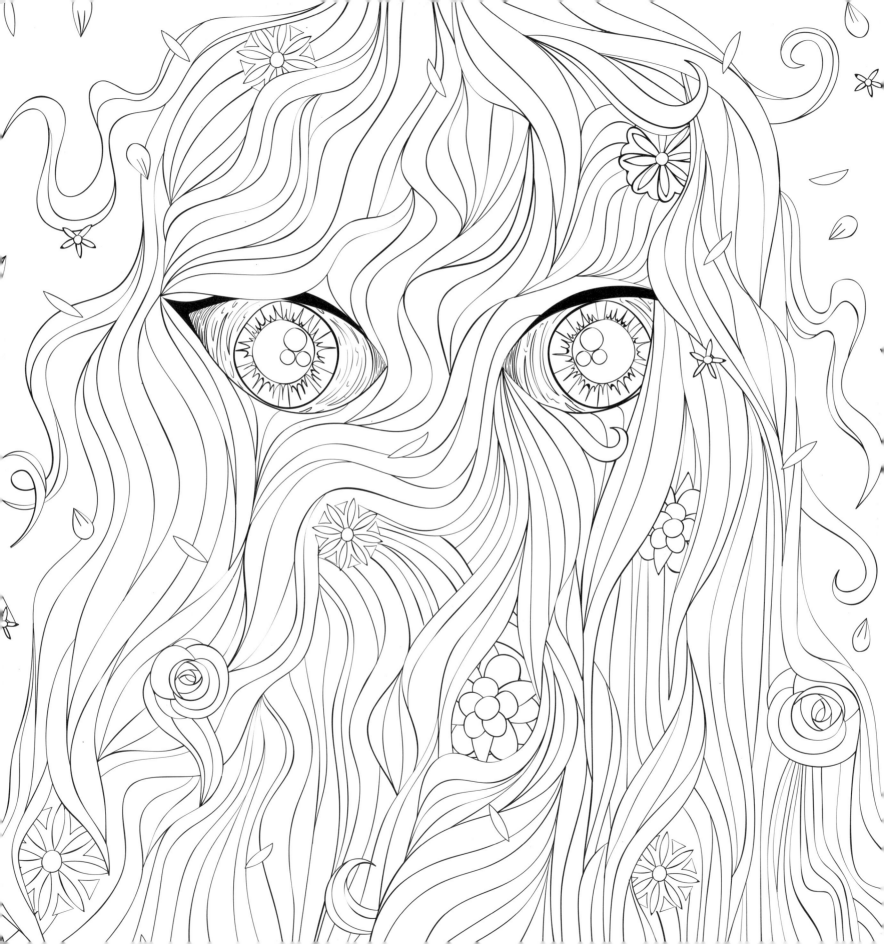

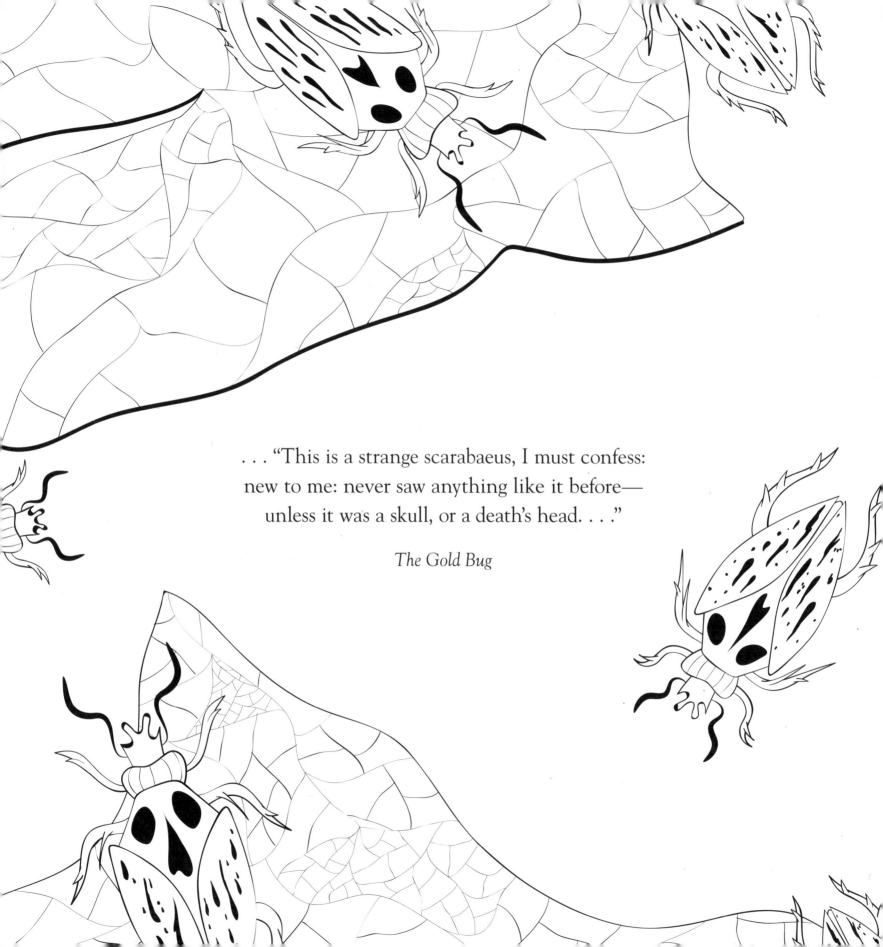

. . . "This is a strange scarabaeus, I must confess:
new to me: never saw anything like it before—
unless it was a skull, or a death's head. . . ."

The Gold Bug

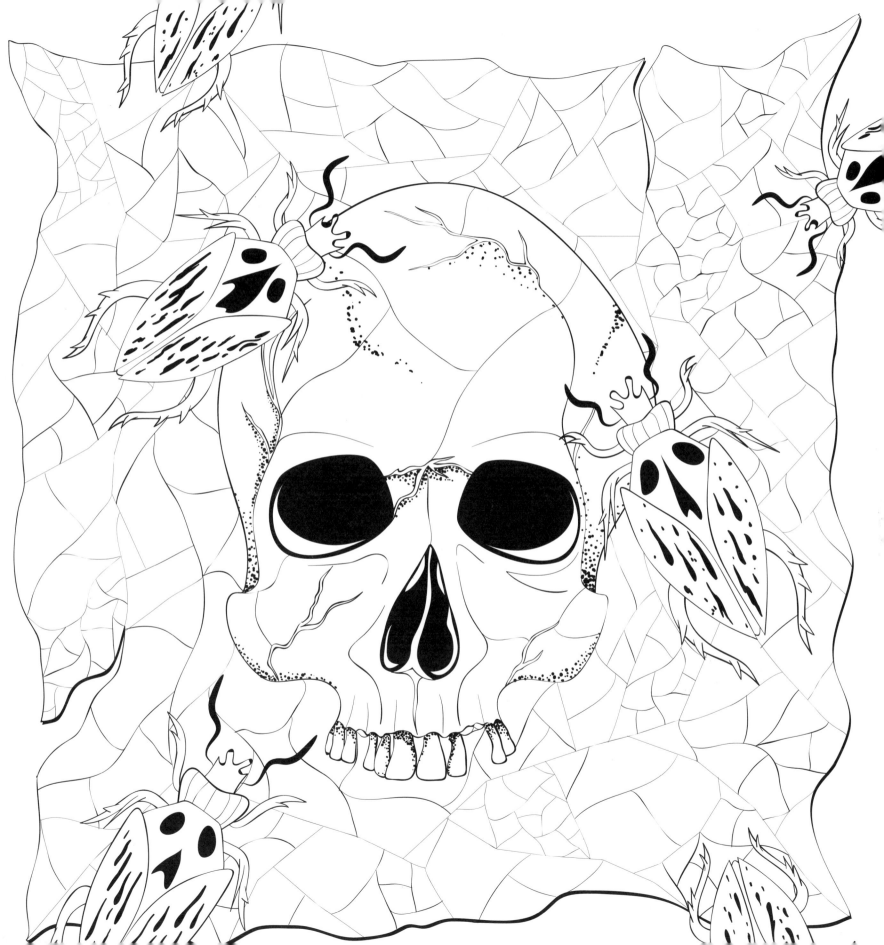

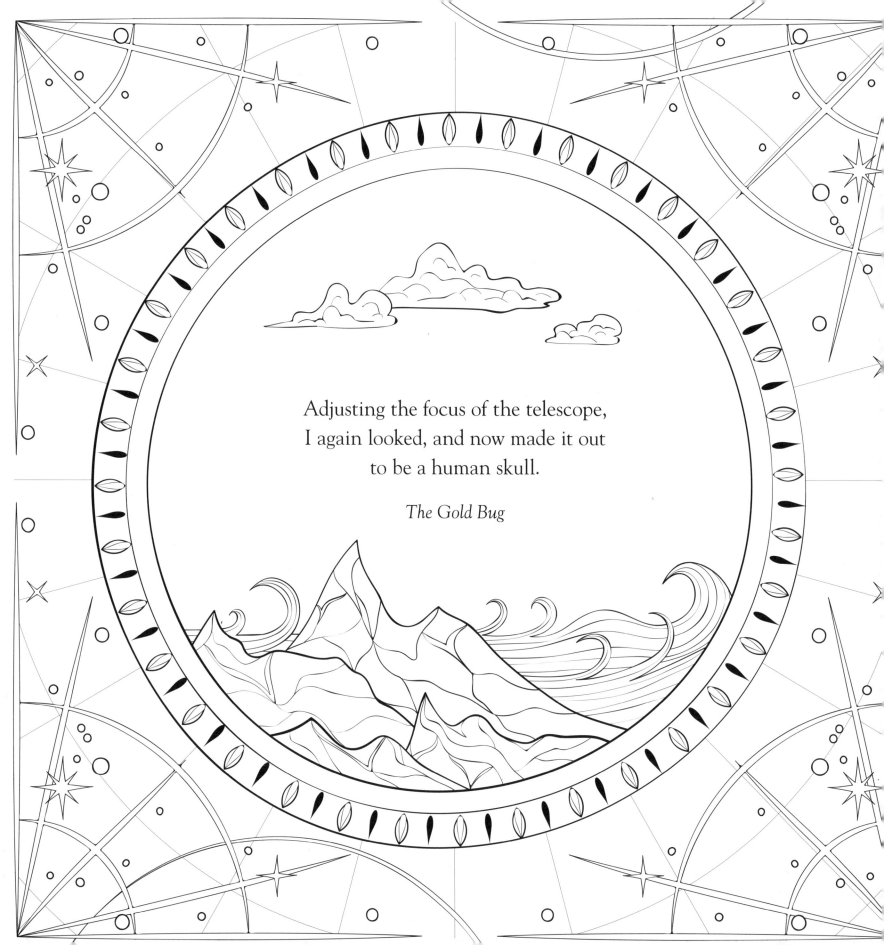

Adjusting the focus of the telescope,
I again looked, and now made it out
to be a human skull.

The Gold Bug

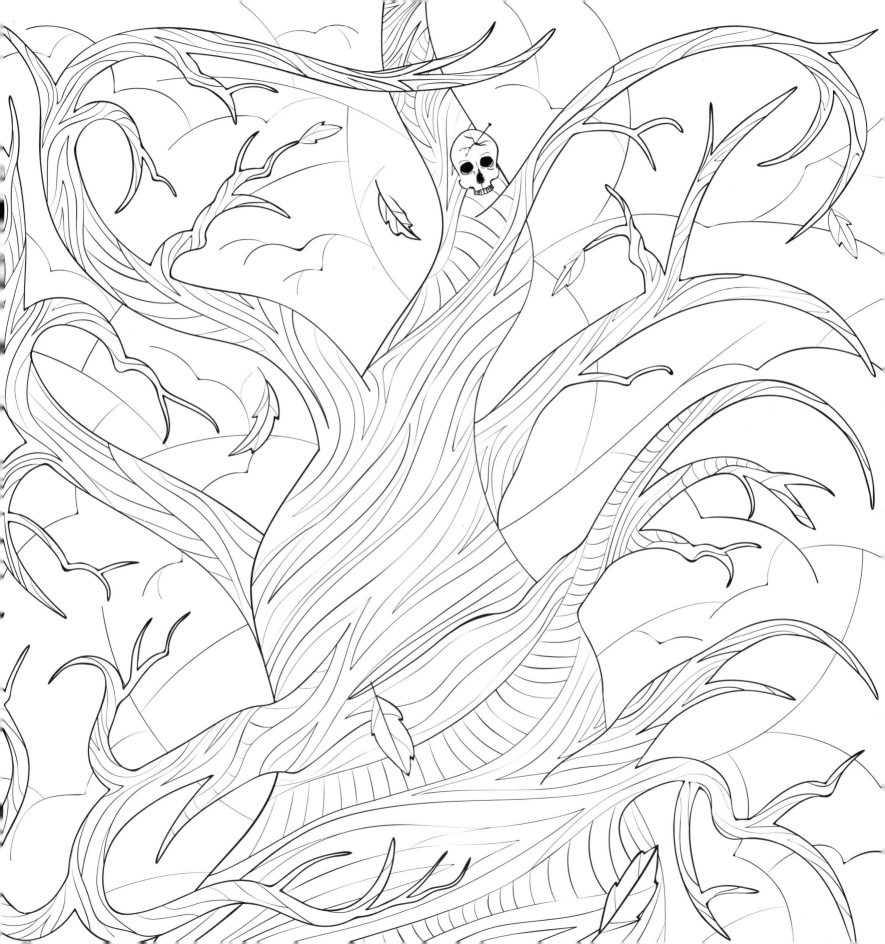

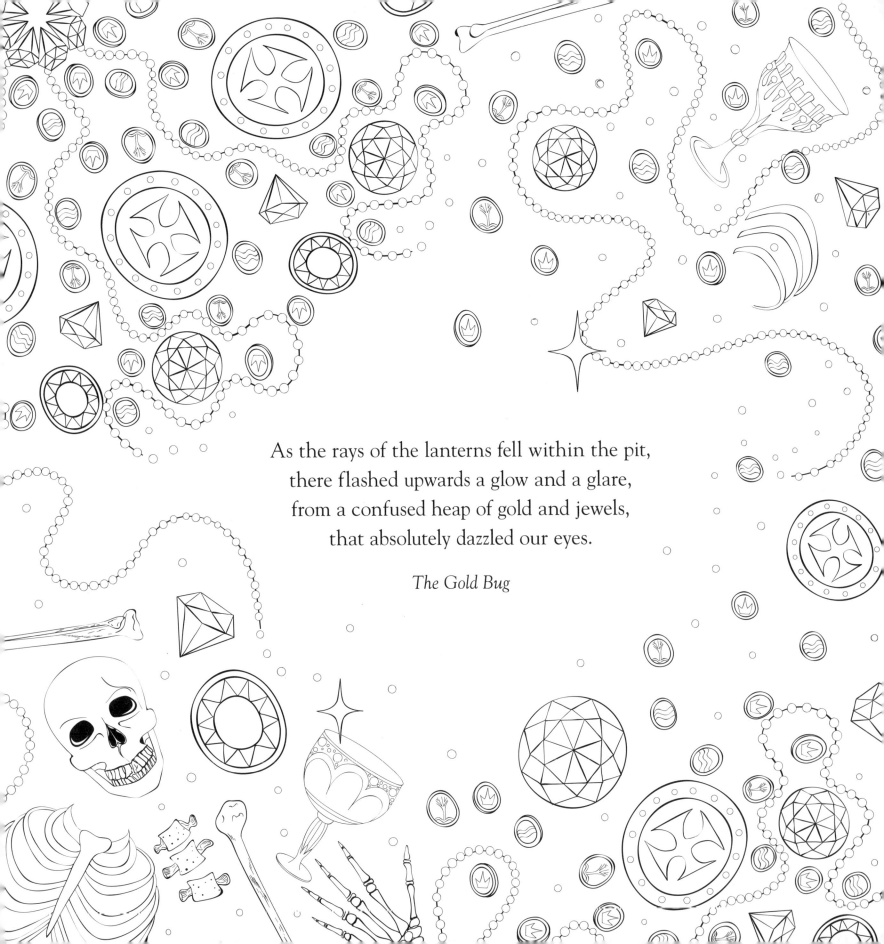

As the rays of the lanterns fell within the pit,
there flashed upwards a glow and a glare,
from a confused heap of gold and jewels,
that absolutely dazzled our eyes.

The Gold Bug

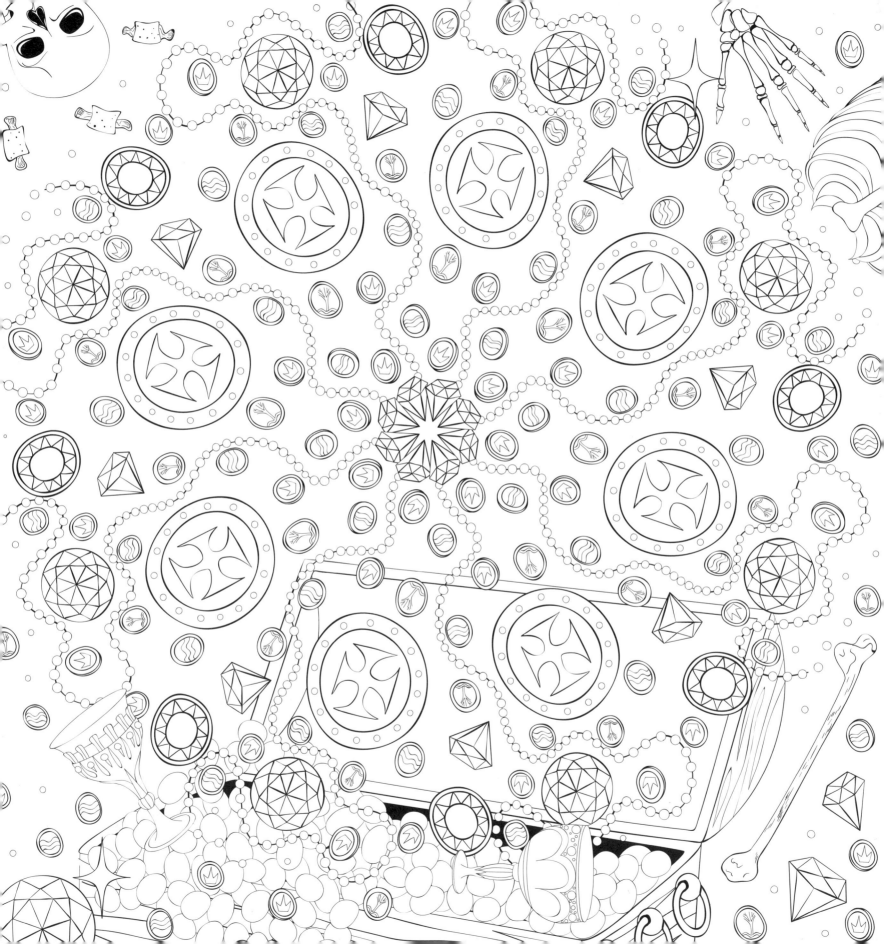

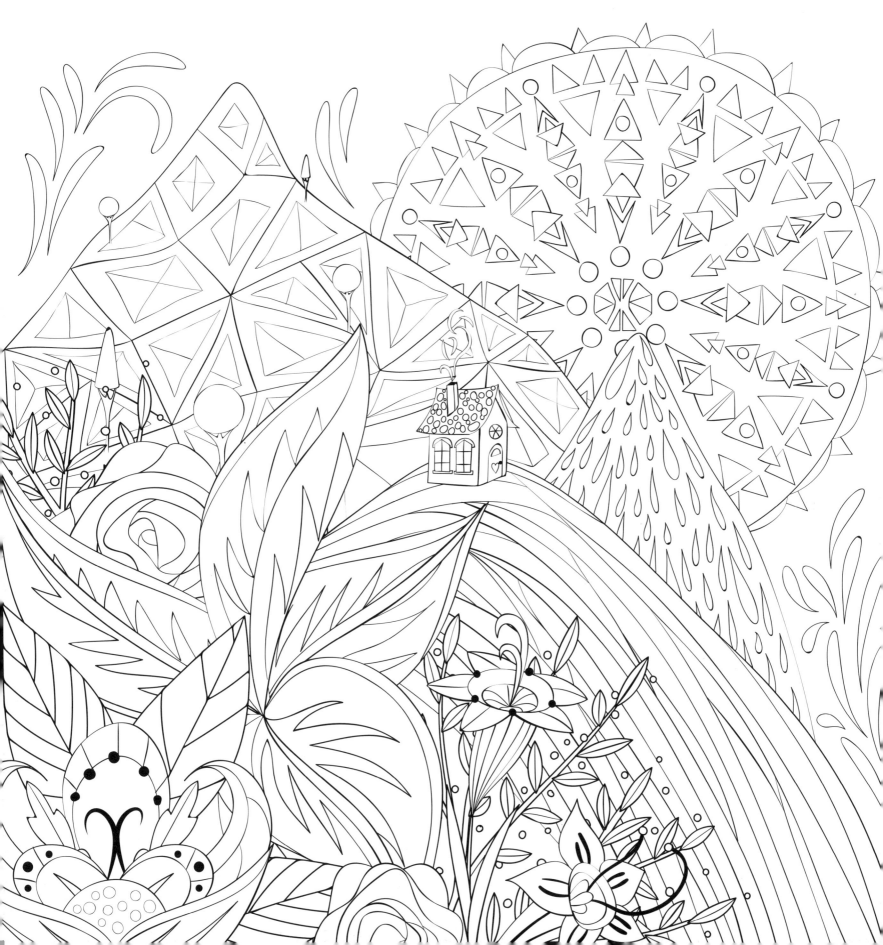

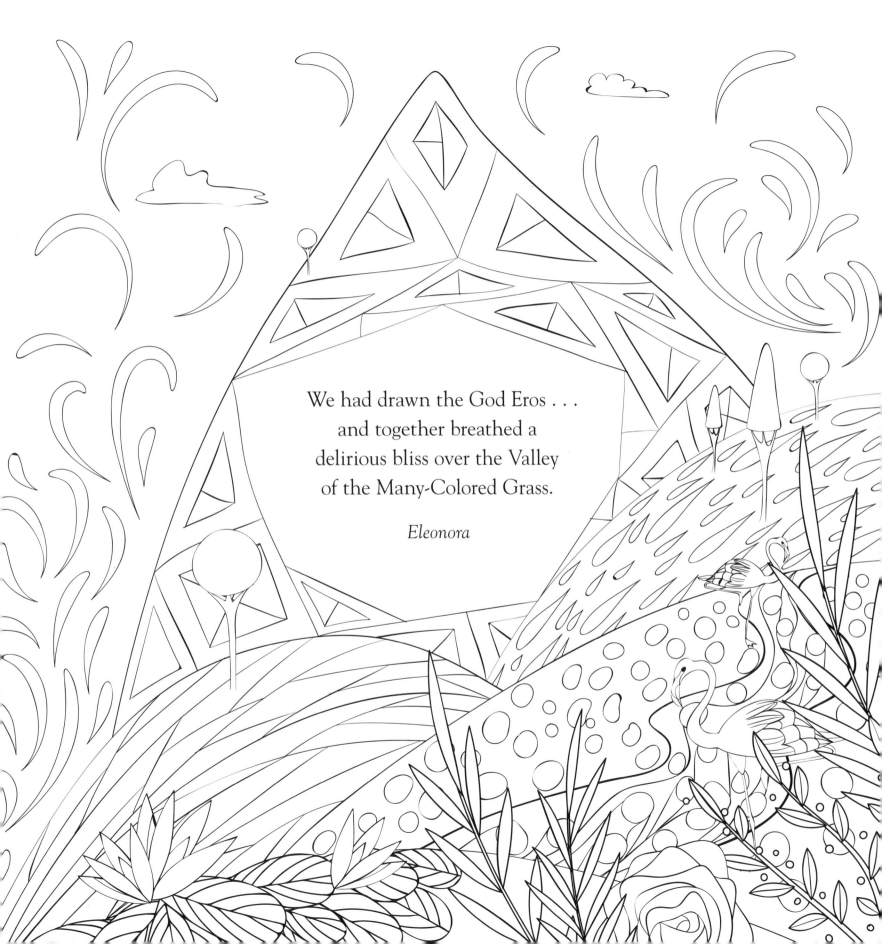

We had drawn the God Eros . . .
and together breathed a
delirious bliss over the Valley
of the Many-Colored Grass.

Eleonora

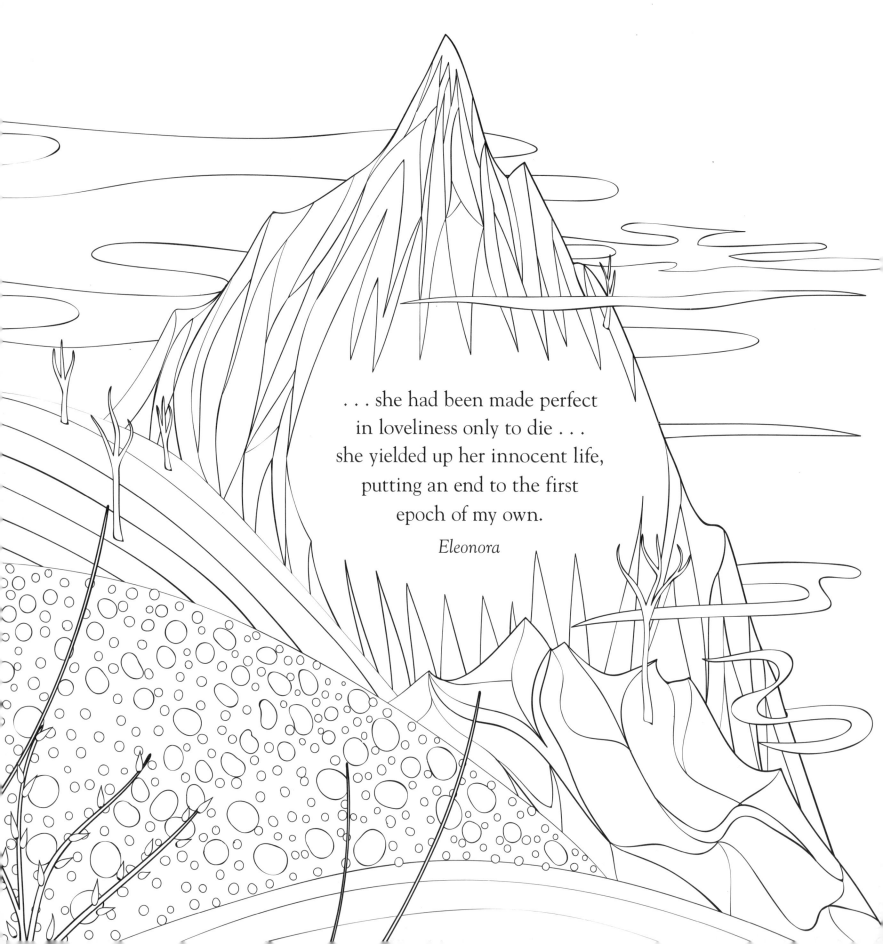

. . . she had been made perfect
in loveliness only to die . . .
she yielded up her innocent life,
putting an end to the first
epoch of my own.

Eleonora

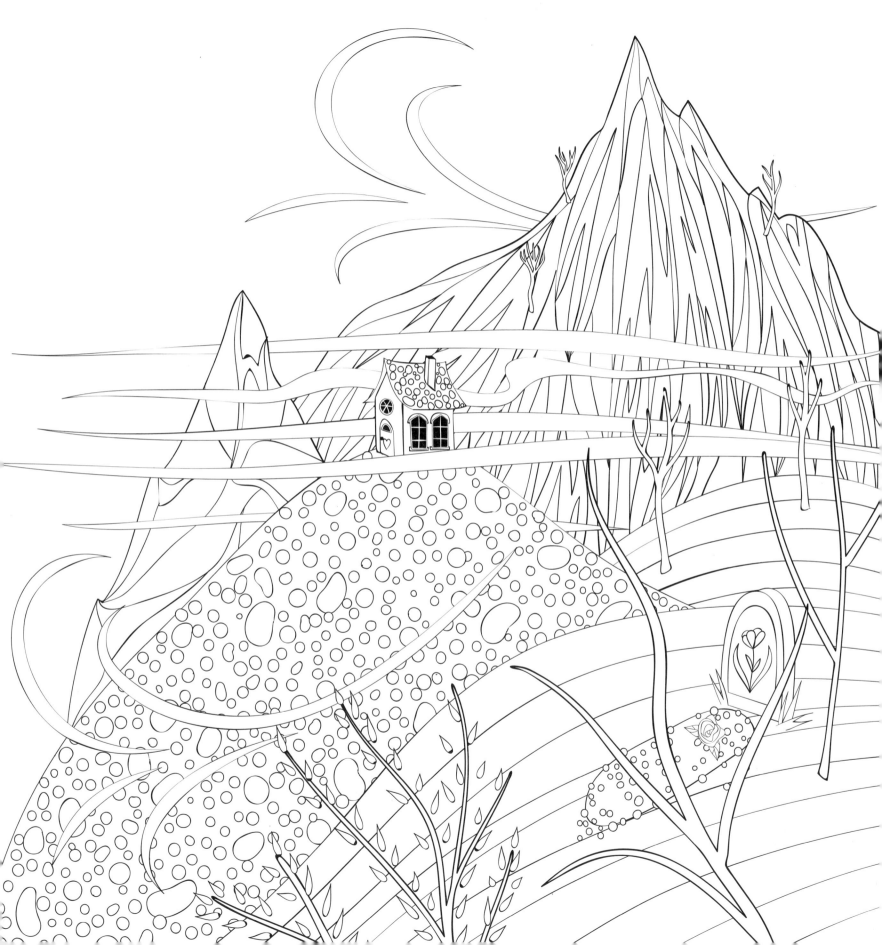

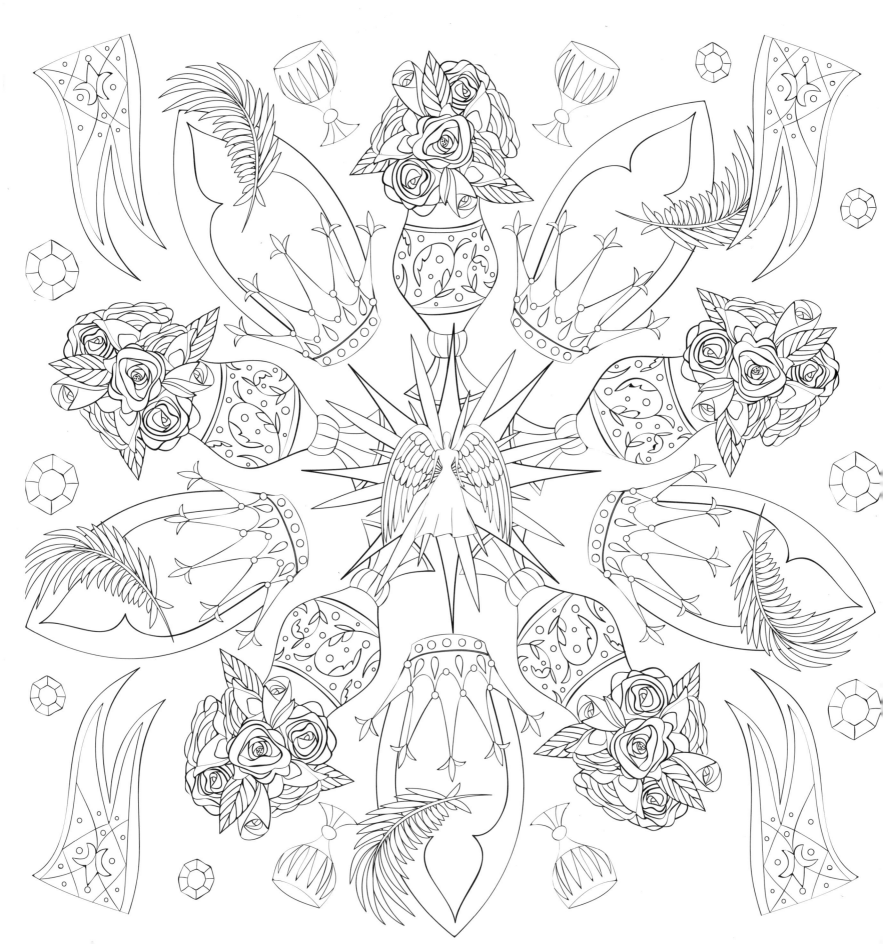

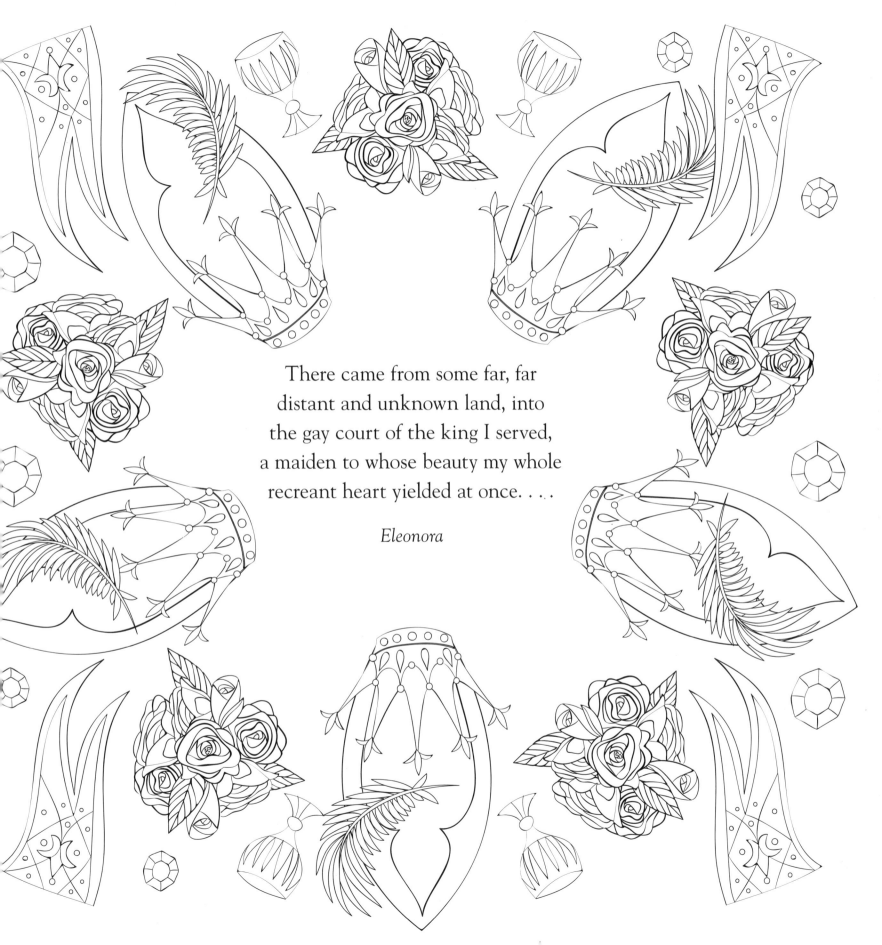

There came from some far, far
distant and unknown land, into
the gay court of the king I served,
a maiden to whose beauty my whole
recreant heart yielded at once. . . .

Eleonora

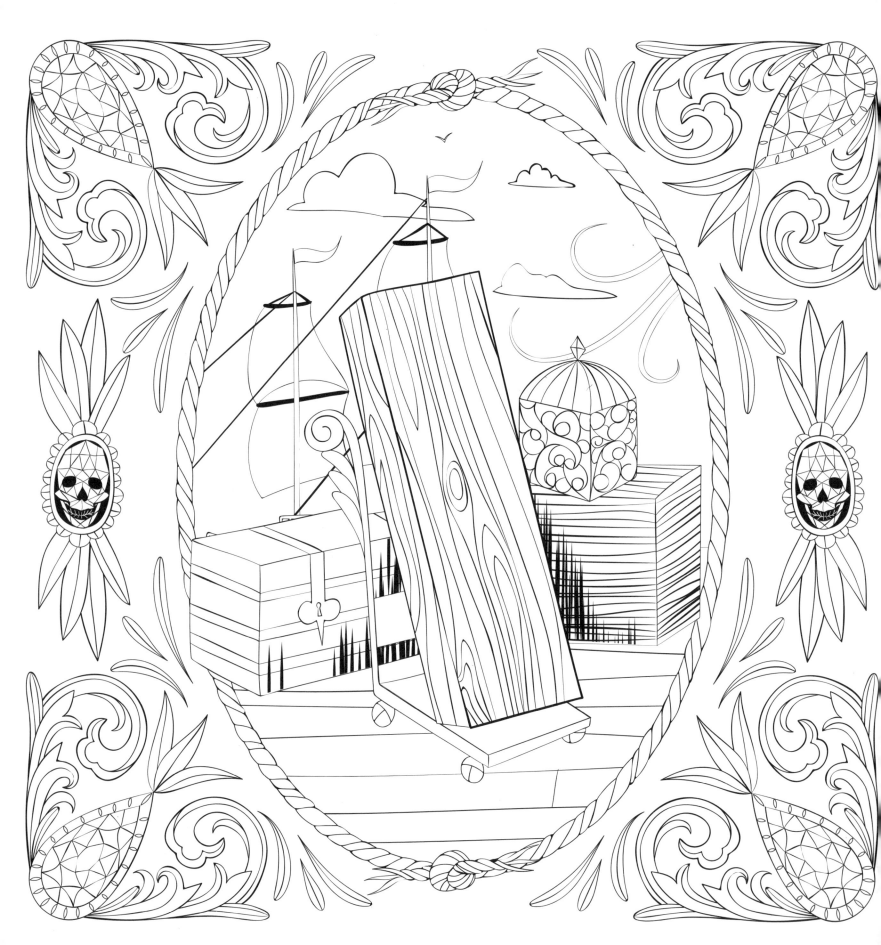

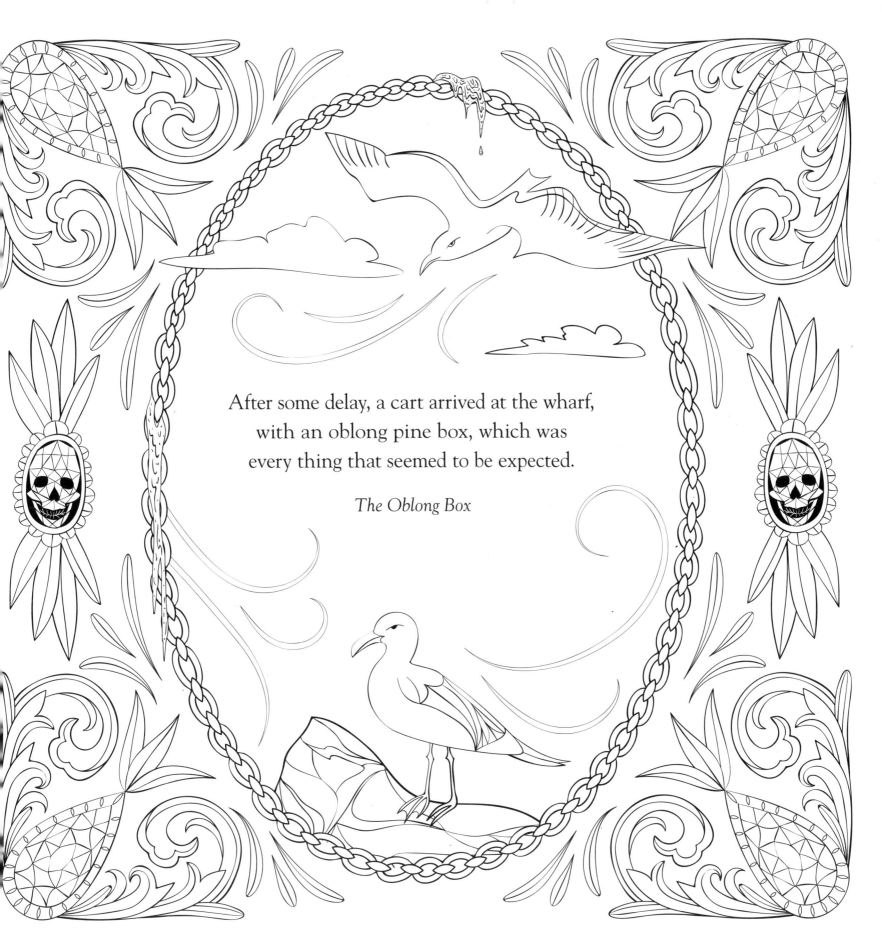

After some delay, a cart arrived at the wharf,
with an oblong pine box, which was
every thing that seemed to be expected.

The Oblong Box

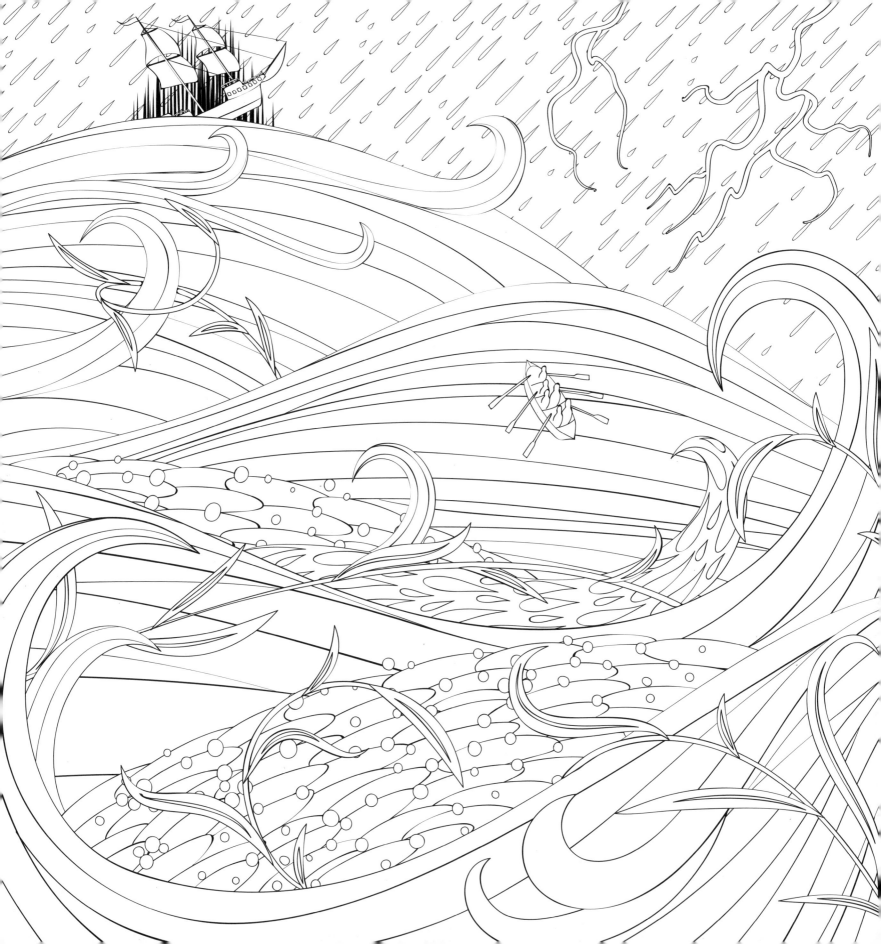

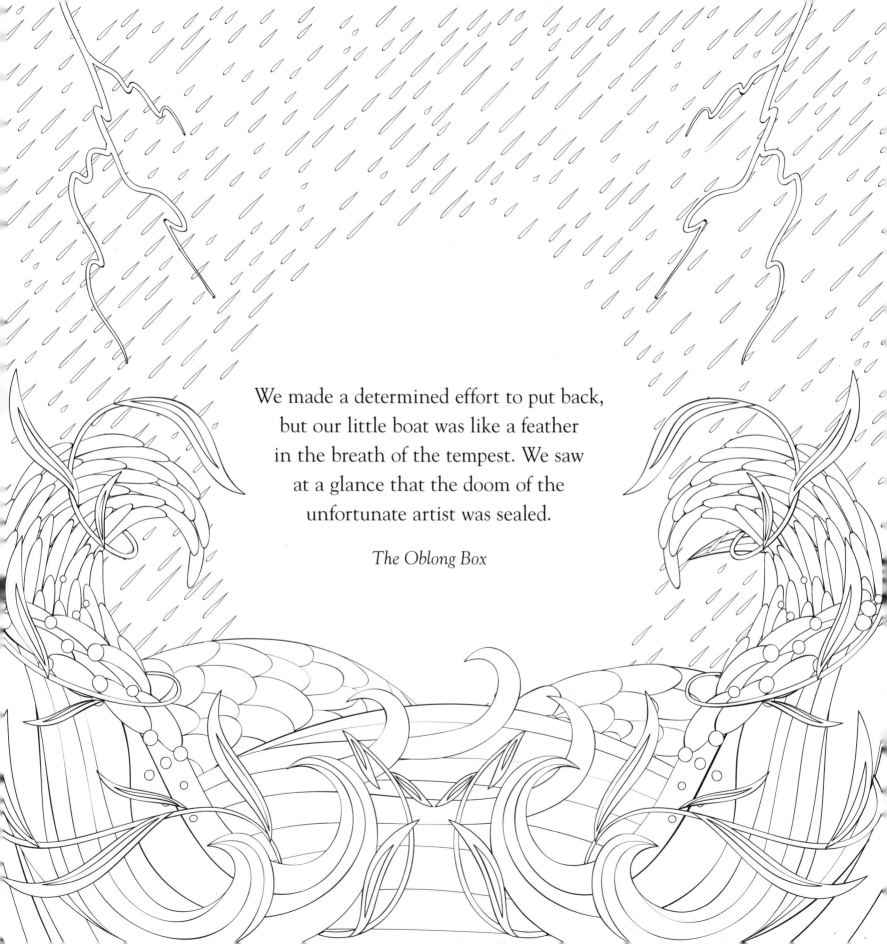

We made a determined effort to put back,
but our little boat was like a feather
in the breath of the tempest. We saw
at a glance that the doom of the
unfortunate artist was sealed.

The Oblong Box

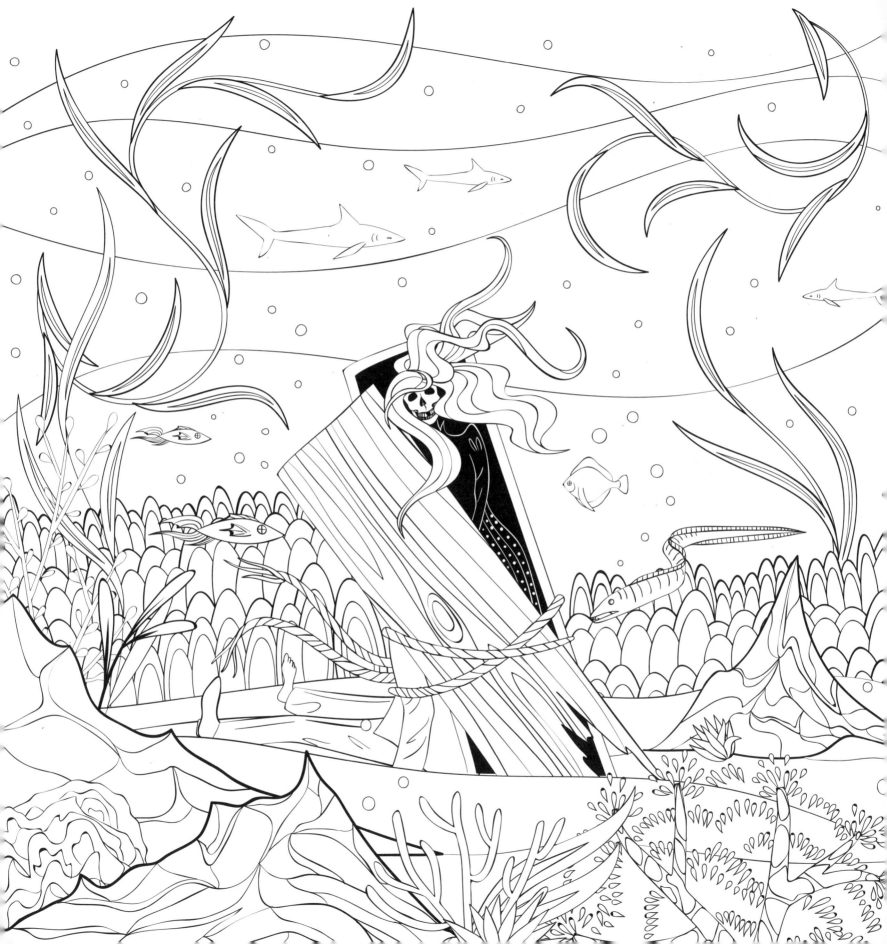

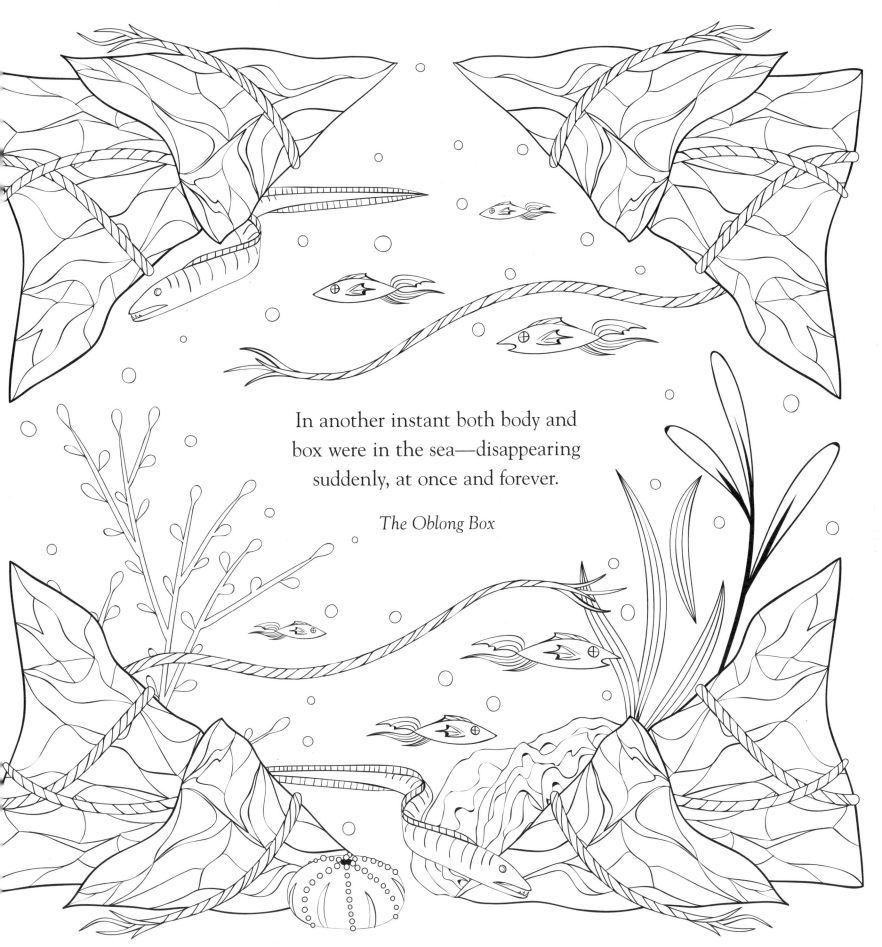

In another instant both body and
box were in the sea—disappearing
suddenly, at once and forever.

The Oblong Box

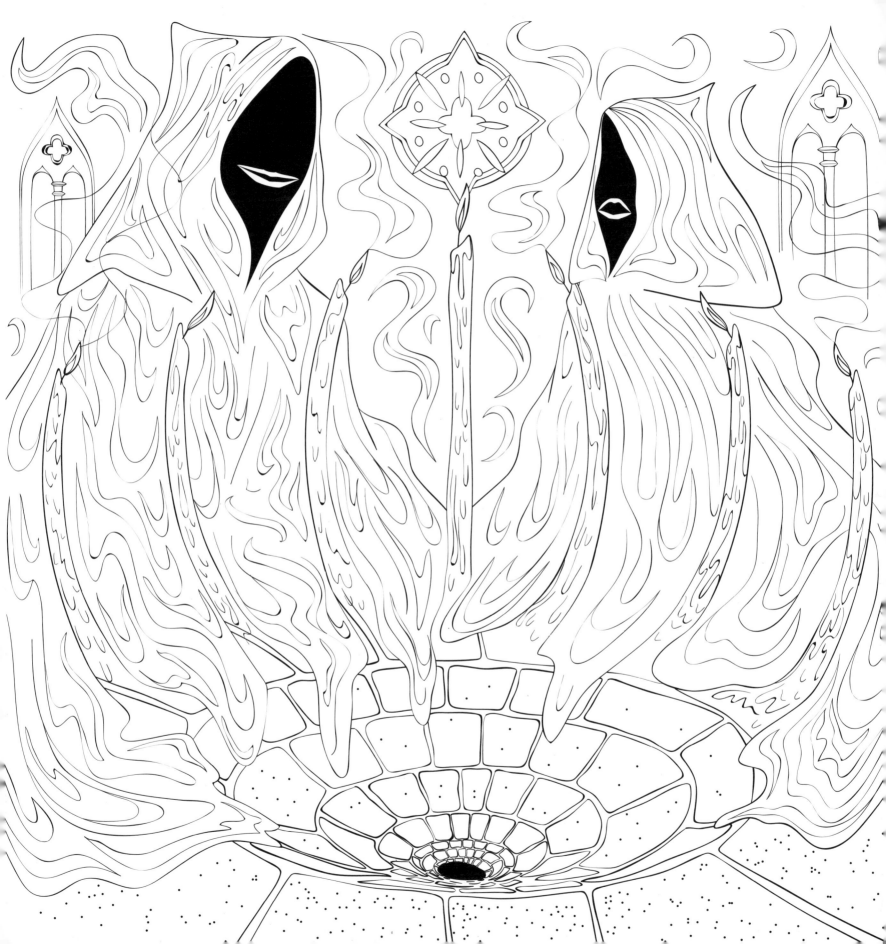

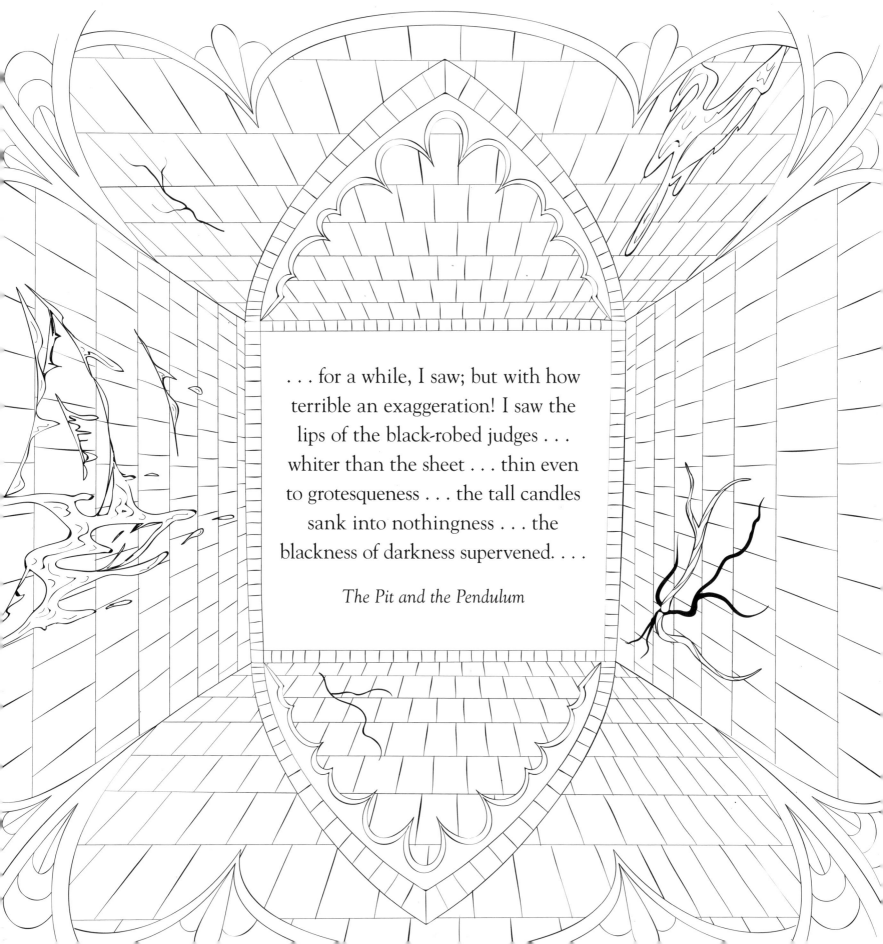

. . . for a while, I saw; but with how
terrible an exaggeration! I saw the
lips of the black-robed judges . . .
whiter than the sheet . . . thin even
to grotesqueness . . . the tall candles
sank into nothingness . . . the
blackness of darkness supervened. . . .

The Pit and the Pendulum

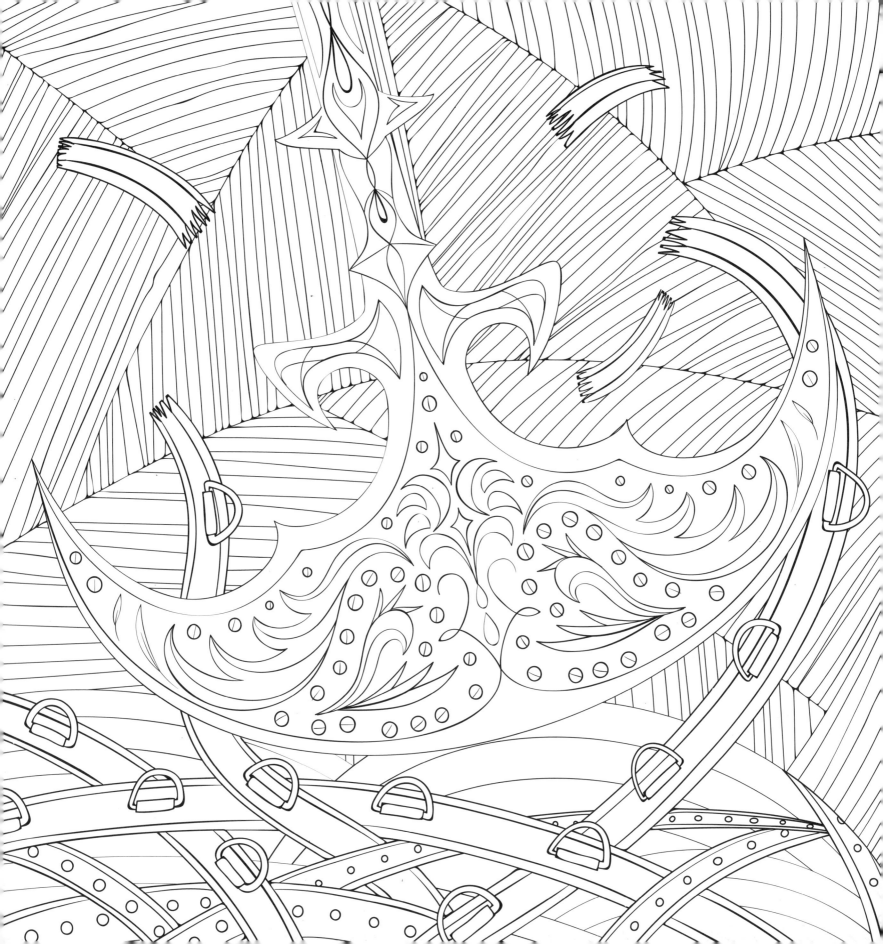

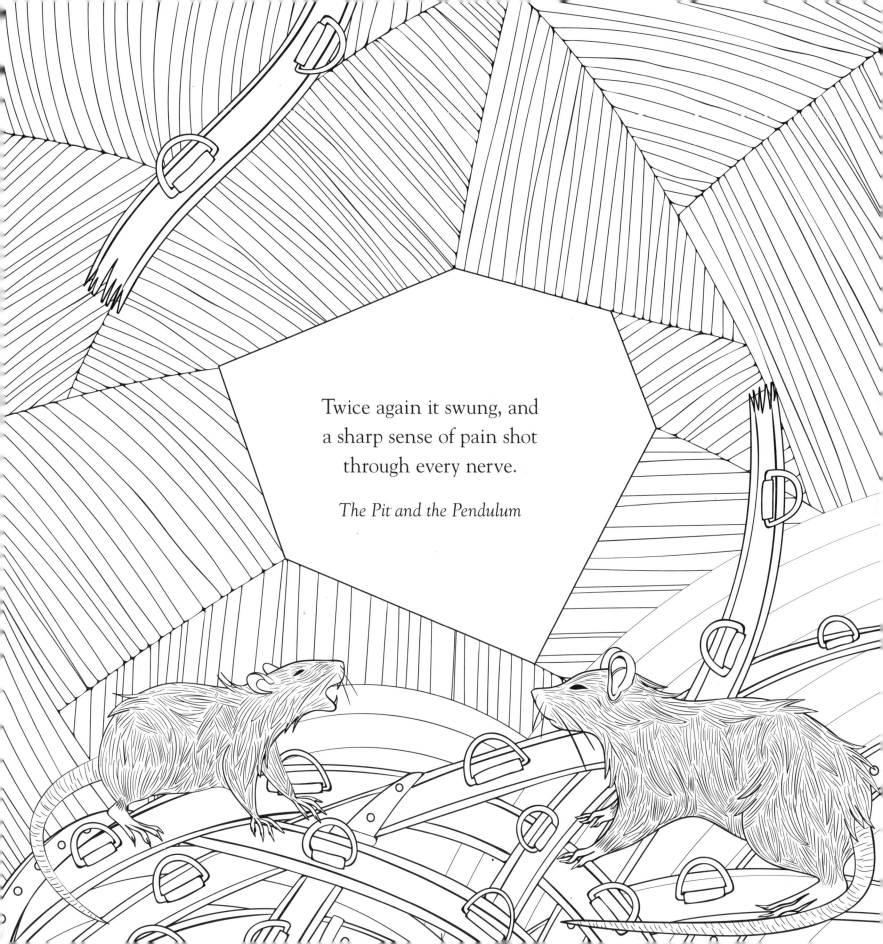

Twice again it swung, and
a sharp sense of pain shot
through every nerve.

The Pit and the Pendulum

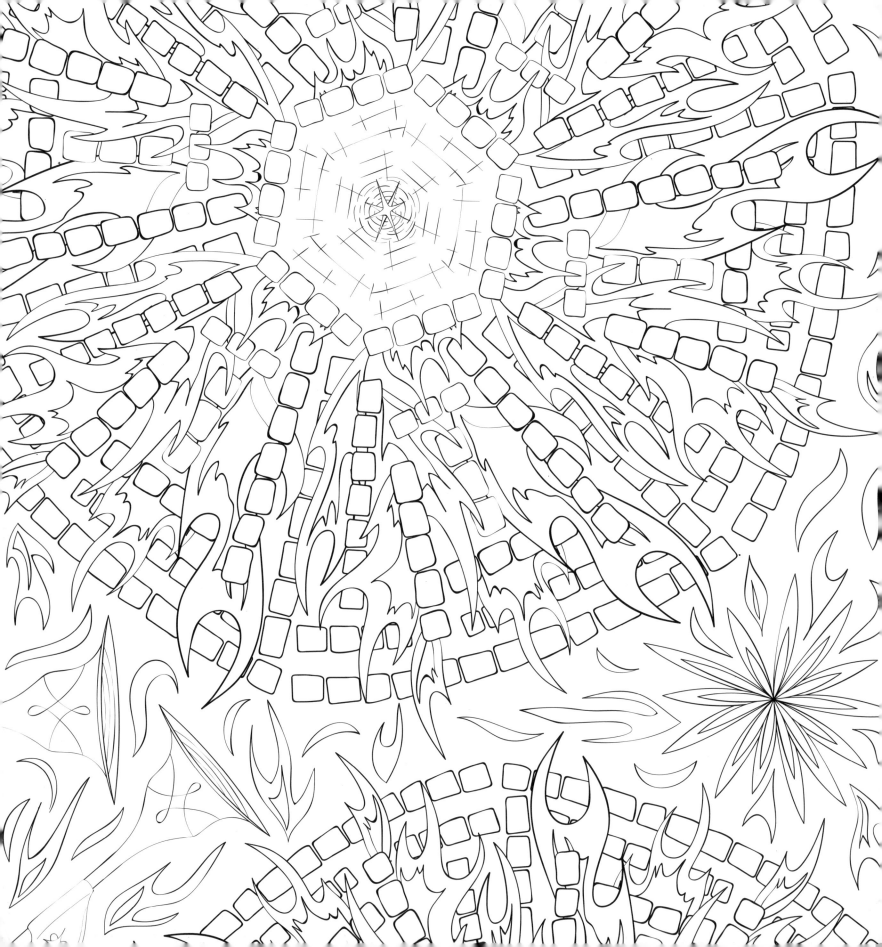

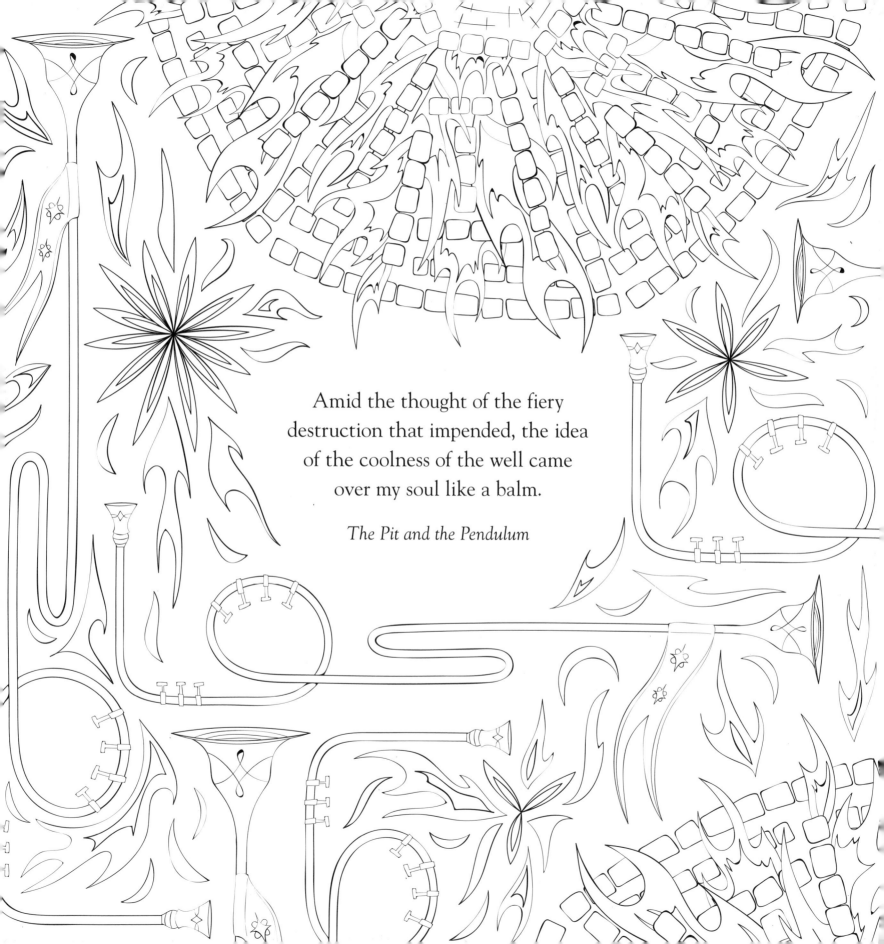

Amid the thought of the fiery
destruction that impended, the idea
of the coolness of the well came
over my soul like a balm.

The Pit and the Pendulum

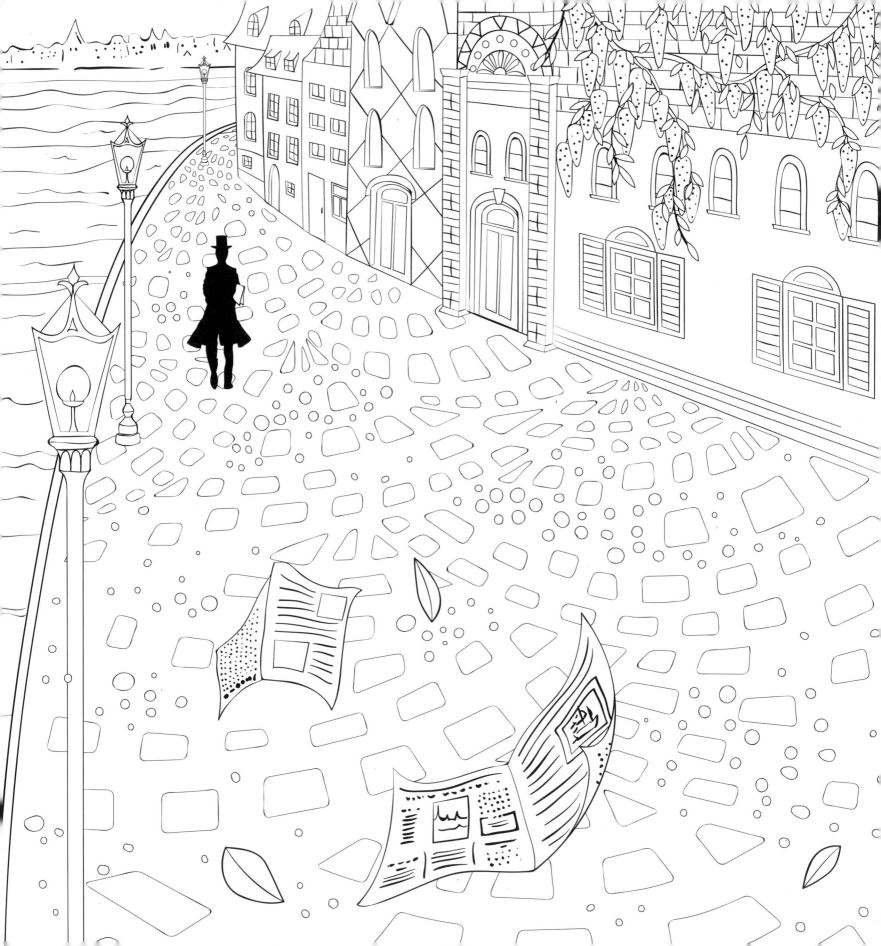

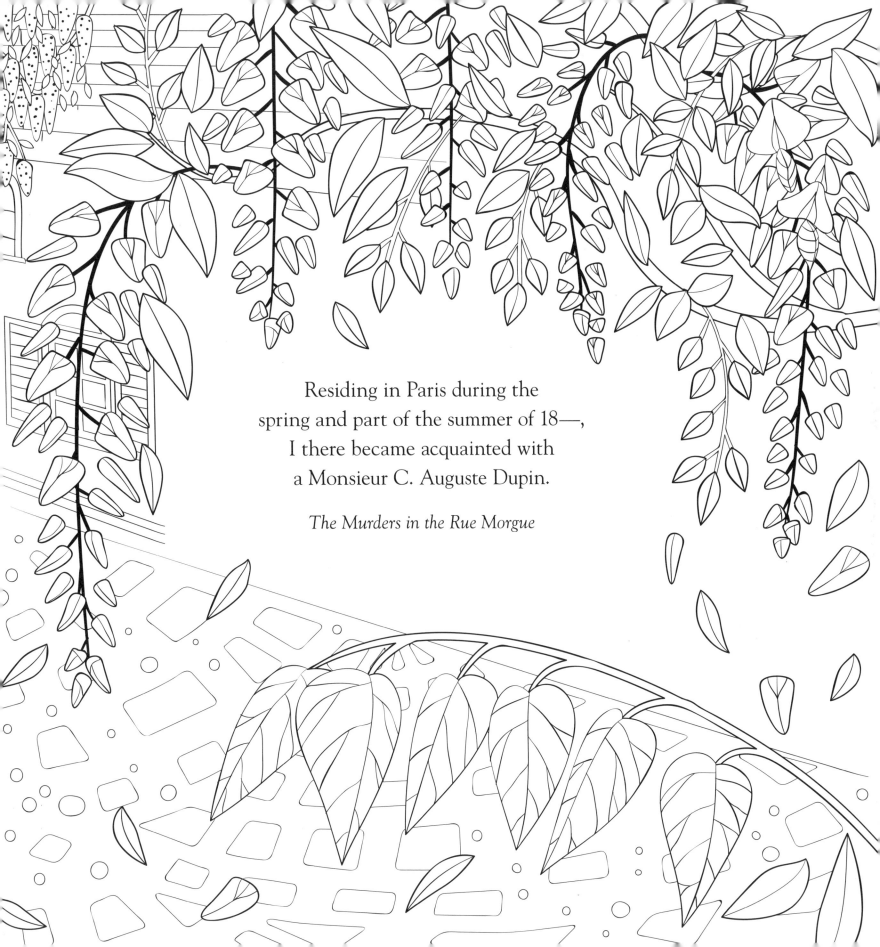

Residing in Paris during the
spring and part of the summer of 18—,
I there became acquainted with
a Monsieur C. Auguste Dupin.

The Murders in the Rue Morgue

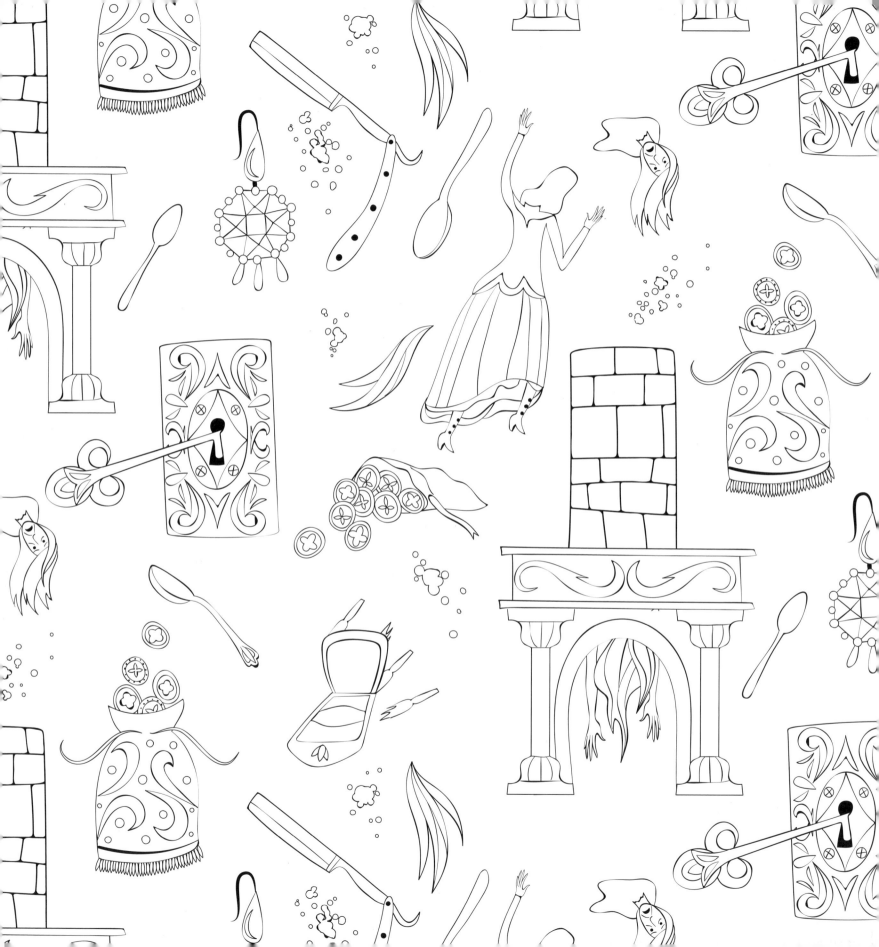

EXTRAORDINARY MURDERS . . .
a spectacle presented itself which
struck every one present not less with
horror than with astonishment.

The Murders in the Rue Morgue

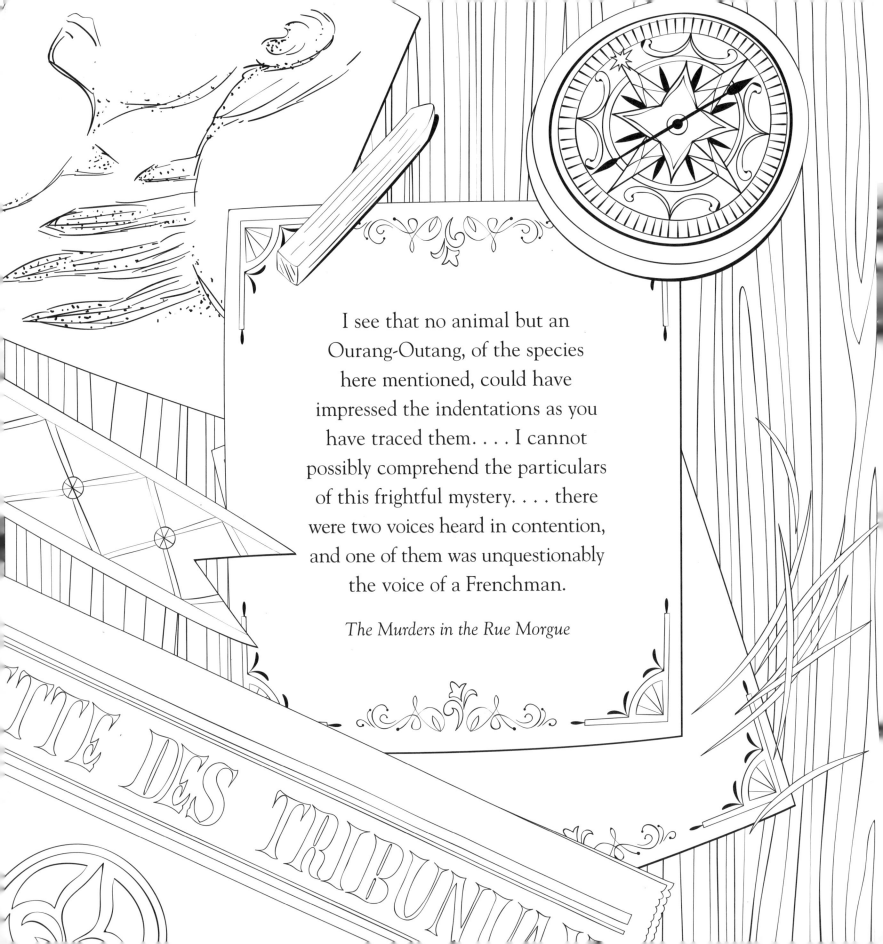

I see that no animal but an
Ourang-Outang, of the species
here mentioned, could have
impressed the indentations as you
have traced them. . . . I cannot
possibly comprehend the particulars
of this frightful mystery. . . . there
were two voices heard in contention,
and one of them was unquestionably
the voice of a Frenchman.

The Murders in the Rue Morgue

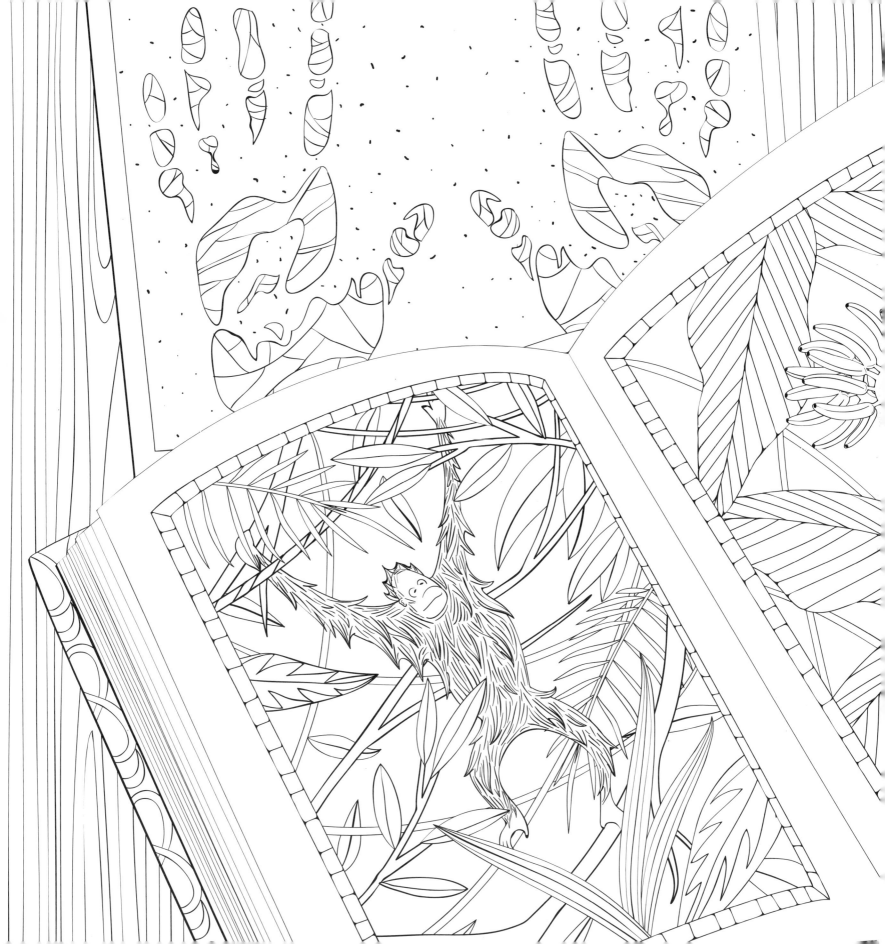

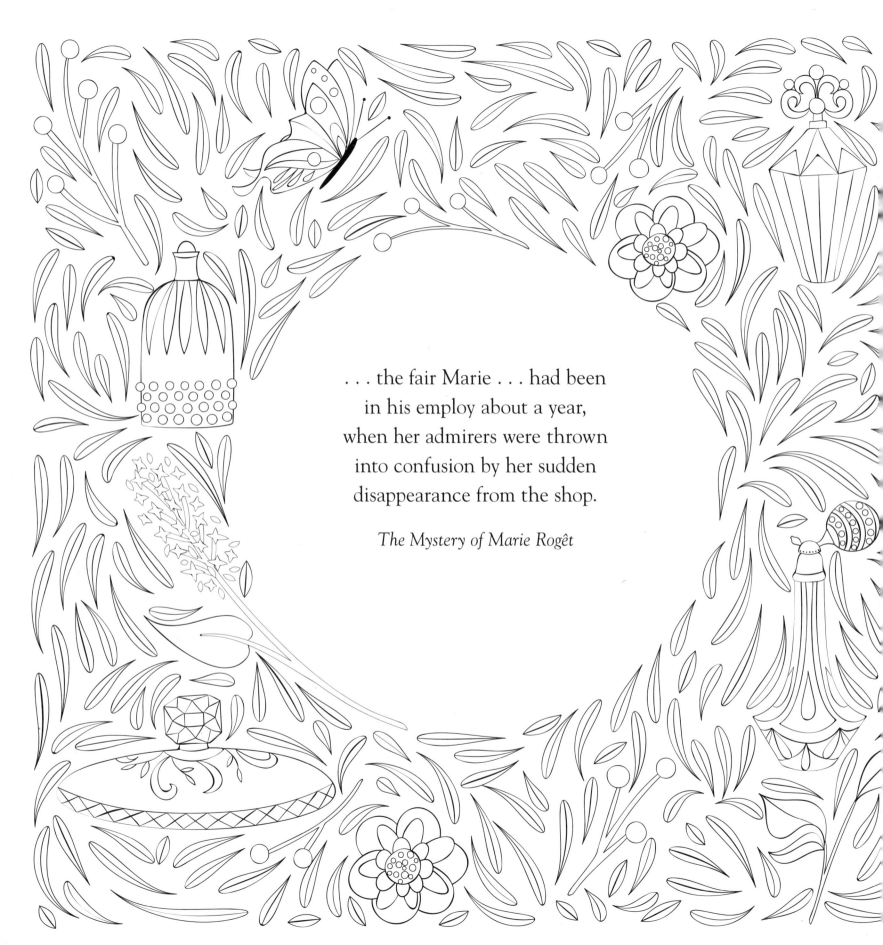

. . . the fair Marie . . . had been
in his employ about a year,
when her admirers were thrown
into confusion by her sudden
disappearance from the shop.

The Mystery of Marie Rogêt

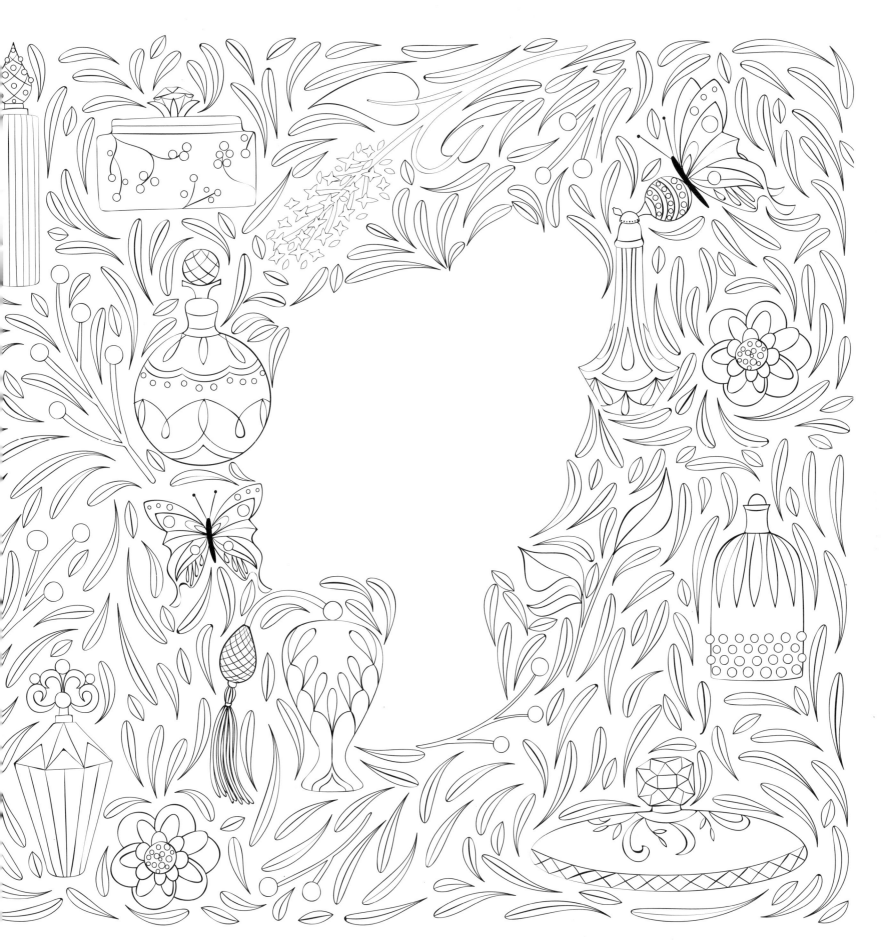

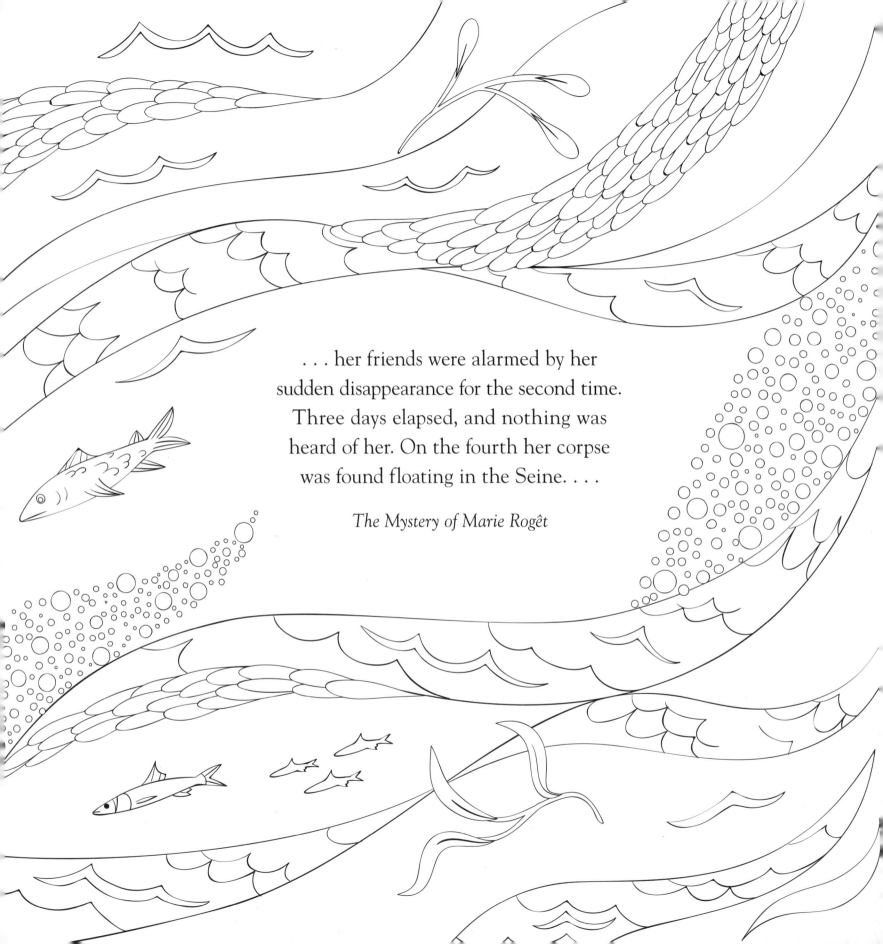

. . . her friends were alarmed by her
sudden disappearance for the second time.
Three days elapsed, and nothing was
heard of her. On the fourth her corpse
was found floating in the Seine. . . .

The Mystery of Marie Rogêt

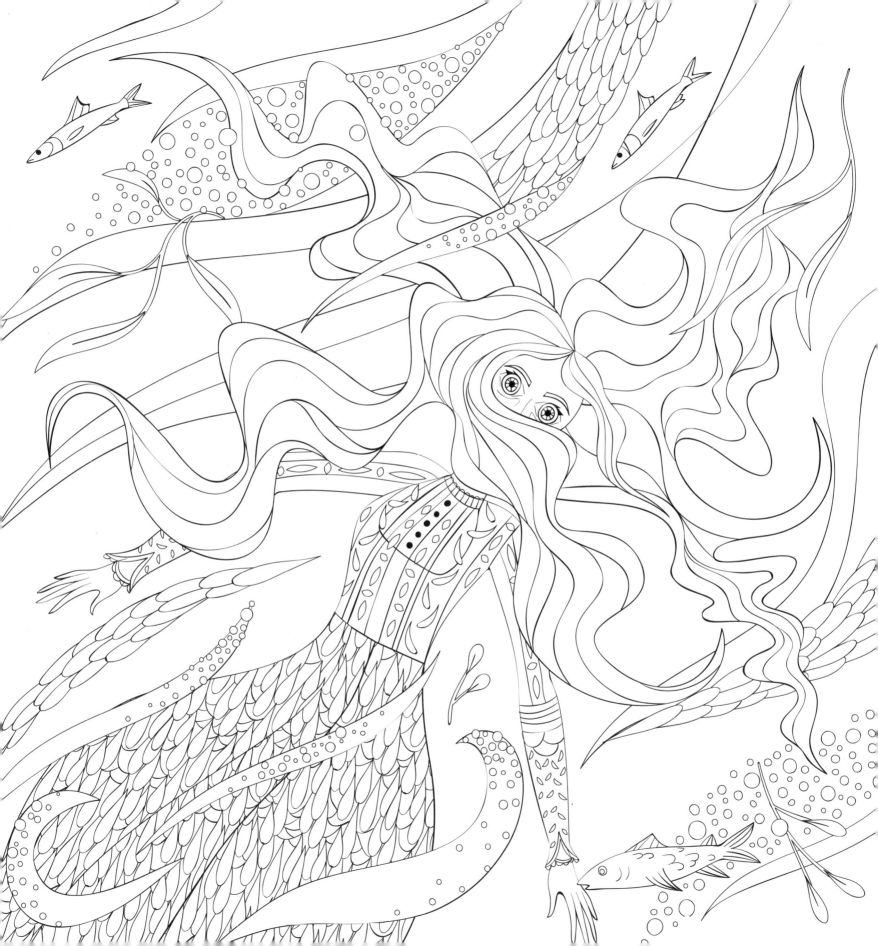

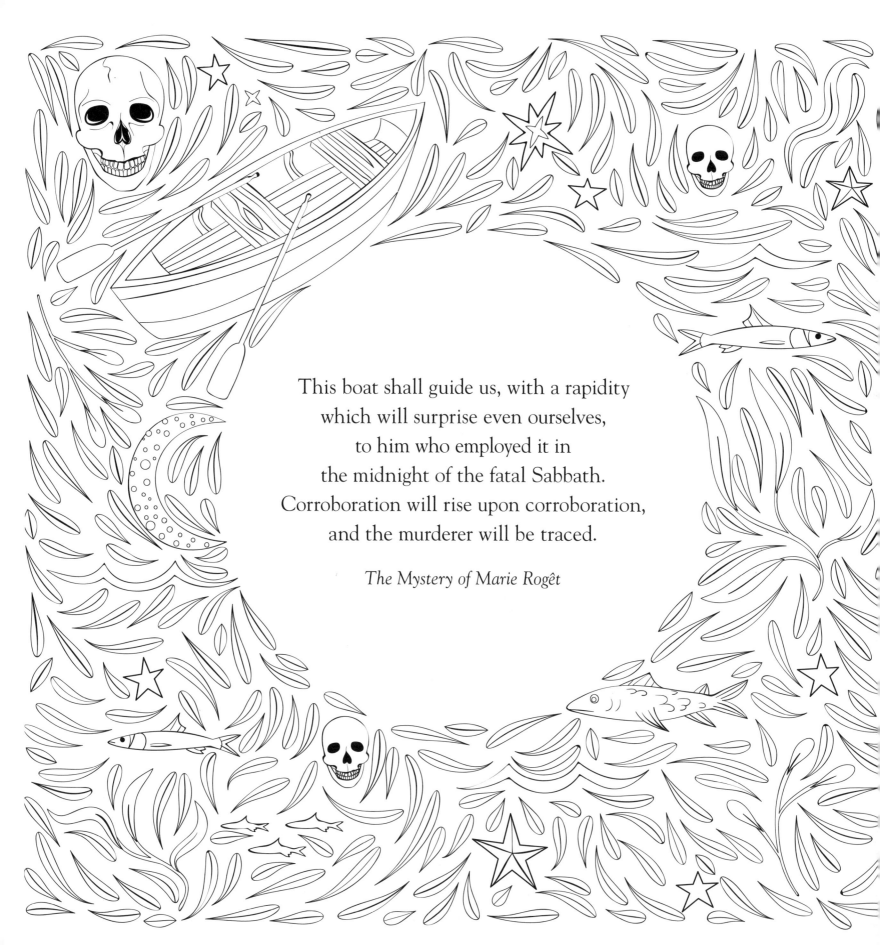

This boat shall guide us, with a rapidity
which will surprise even ourselves,
to him who employed it in
the midnight of the fatal Sabbath.
Corroboration will rise upon corroboration,
and the murderer will be traced.

The Mystery of Marie Rogêt

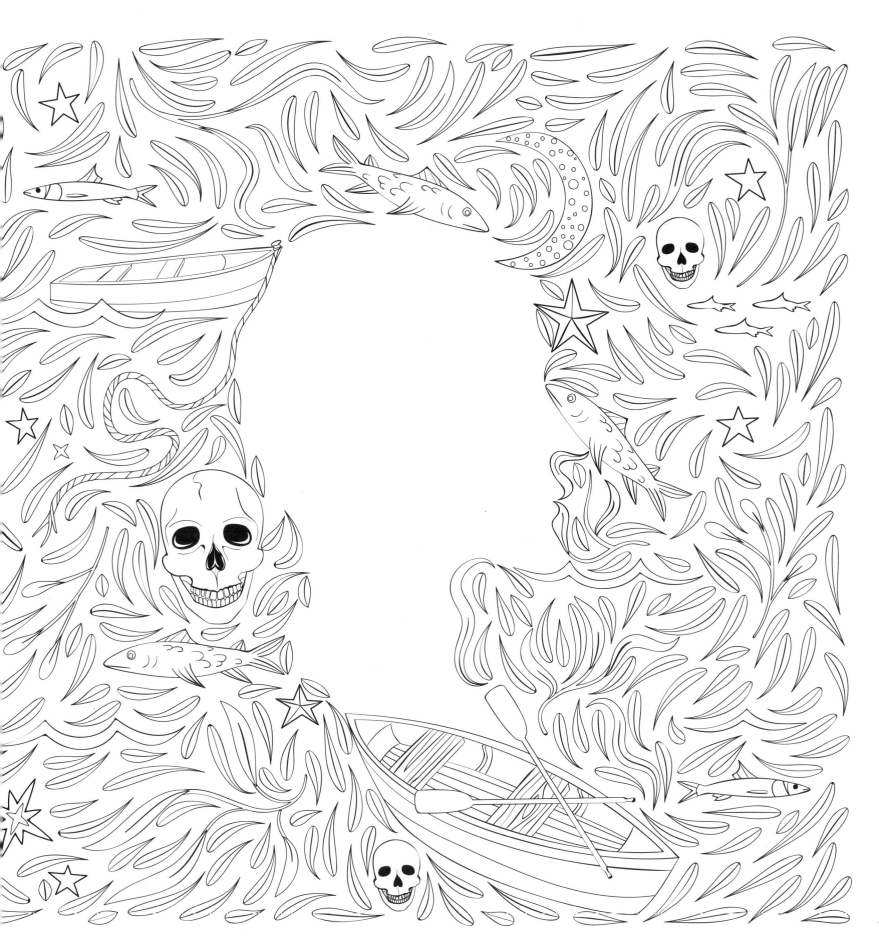

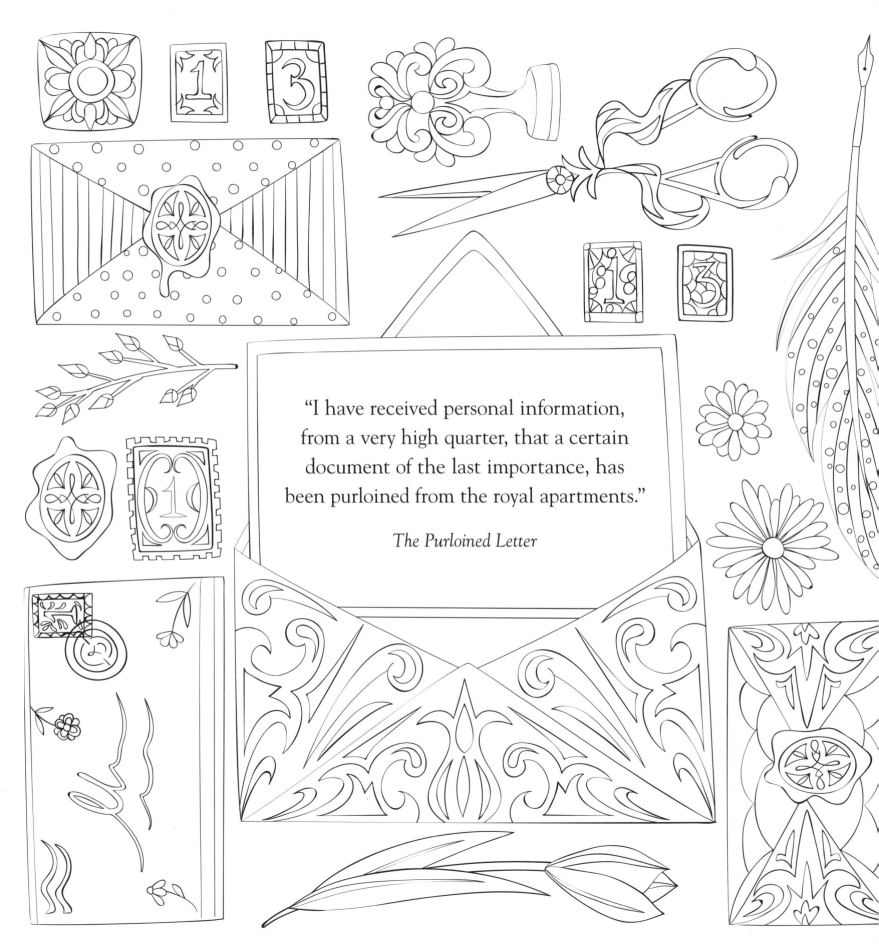

"I have received personal information, from a very high quarter, that a certain document of the last importance, has been purloined from the royal apartments."

The Purloined Letter

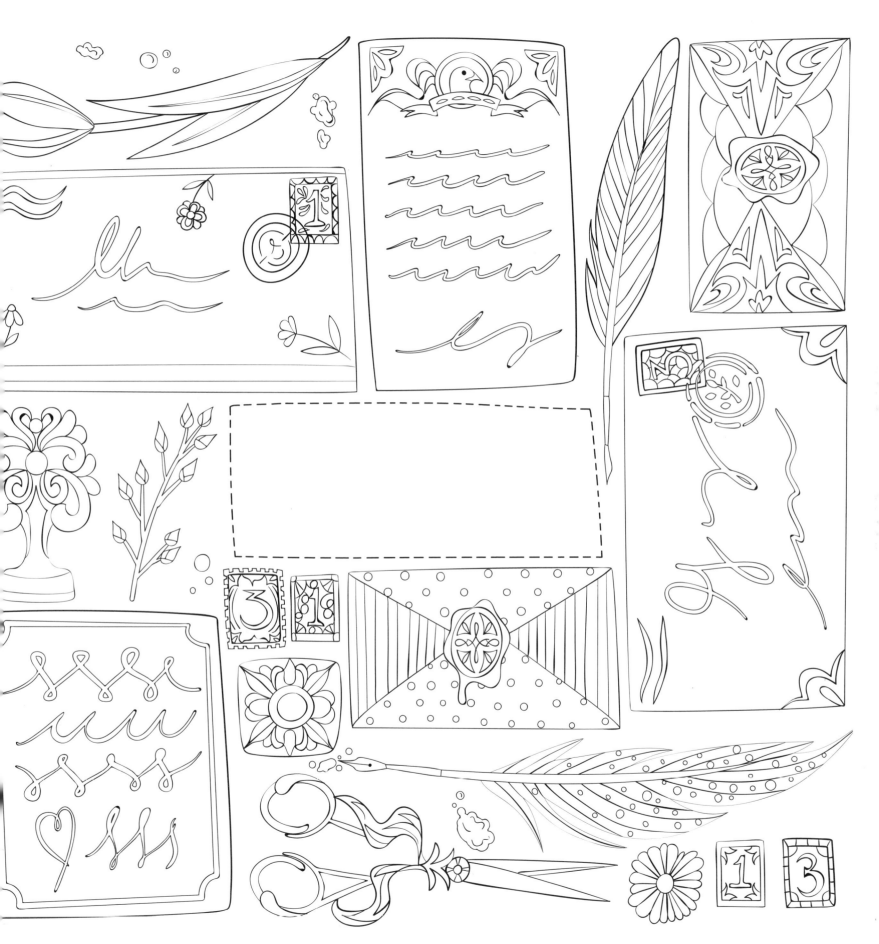

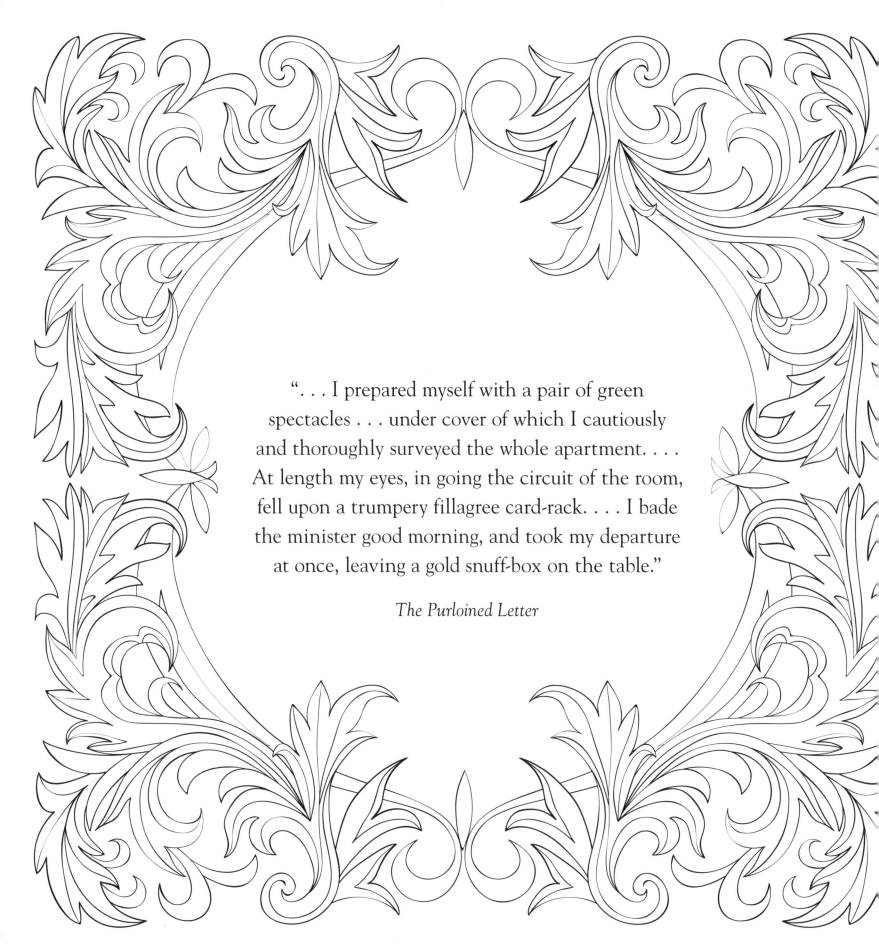

"... I prepared myself with a pair of green spectacles ... under cover of which I cautiously and thoroughly surveyed the whole apartment. ... At length my eyes, in going the circuit of the room, fell upon a trumpery fillagree card-rack. ... I bade the minister good morning, and took my departure at once, leaving a gold snuff-box on the table."

The Purloined Letter

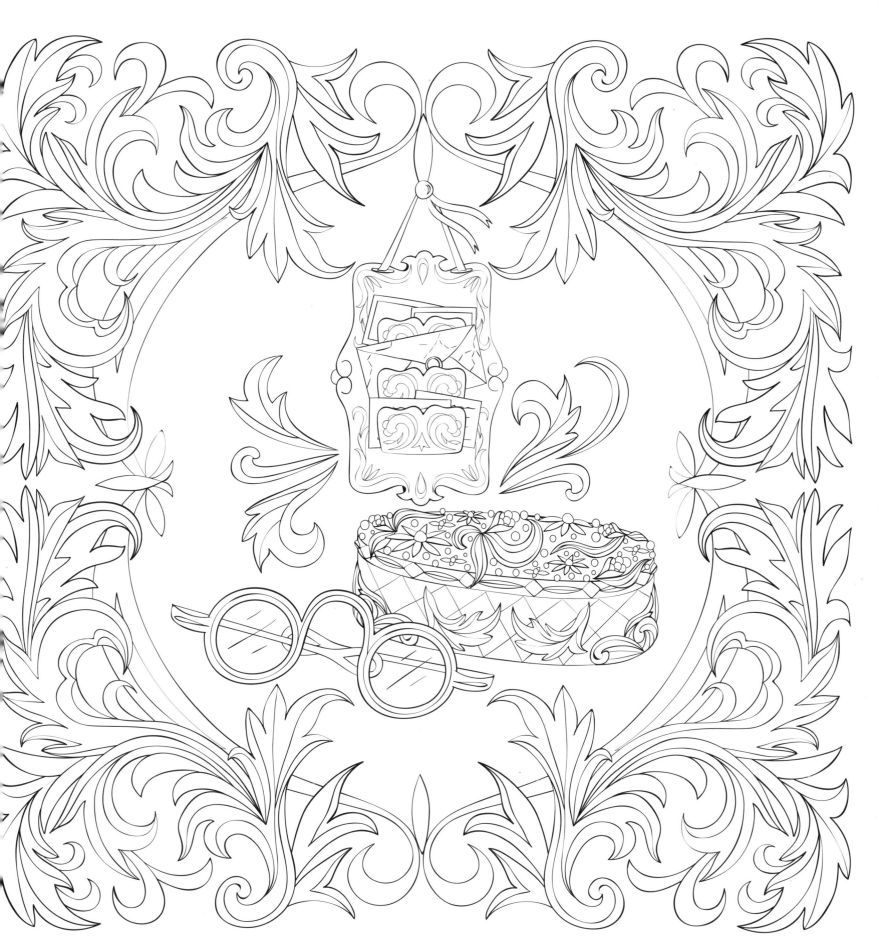

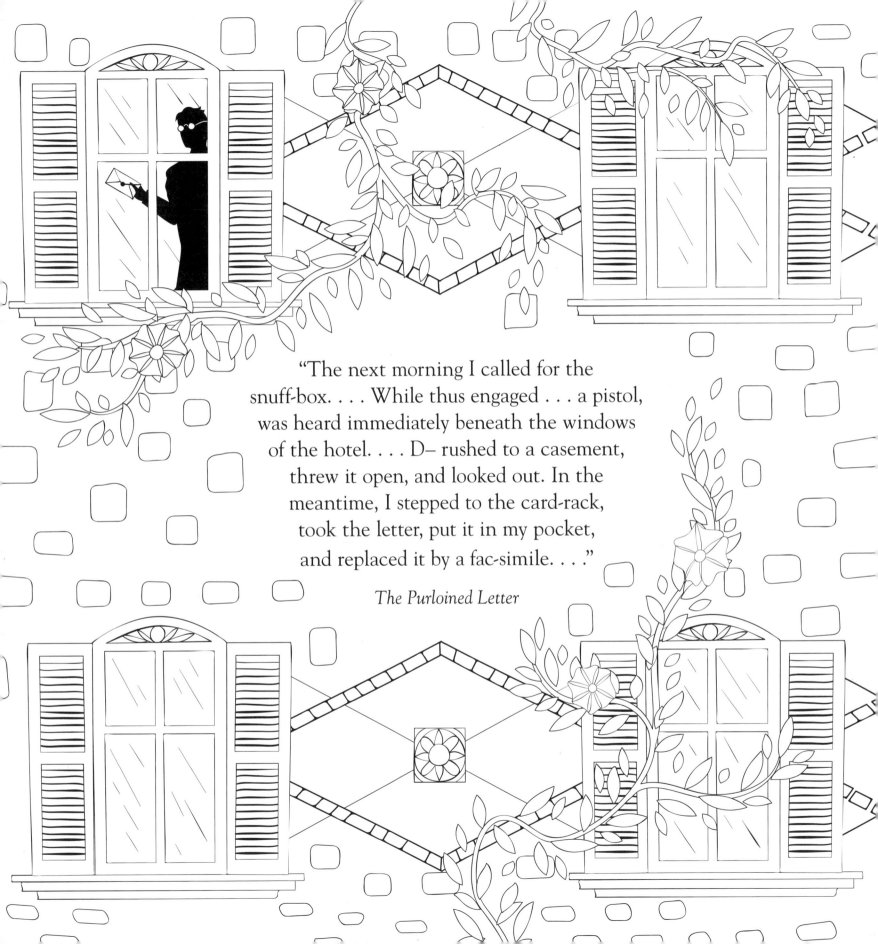

"The next morning I called for the
snuff-box. . . . While thus engaged . . . a pistol,
was heard immediately beneath the windows
of the hotel. . . . D– rushed to a casement,
threw it open, and looked out. In the
meantime, I stepped to the card-rack,
took the letter, put it in my pocket,
and replaced it by a fac-simile. . . ."

The Purloined Letter

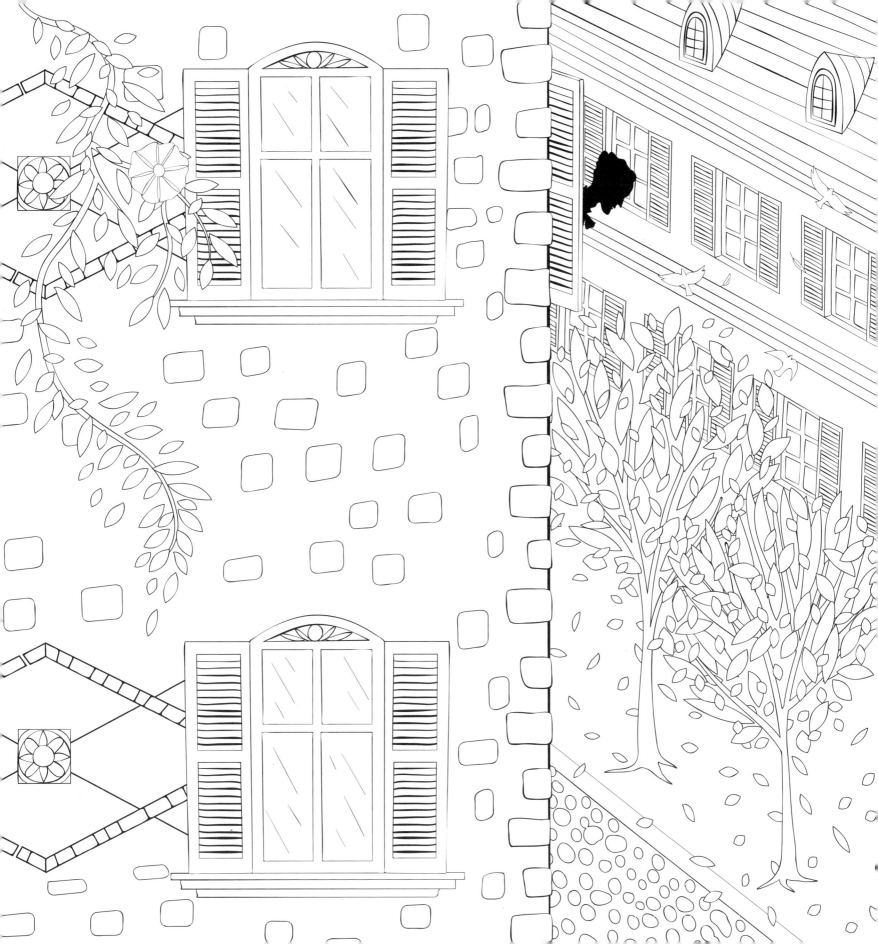

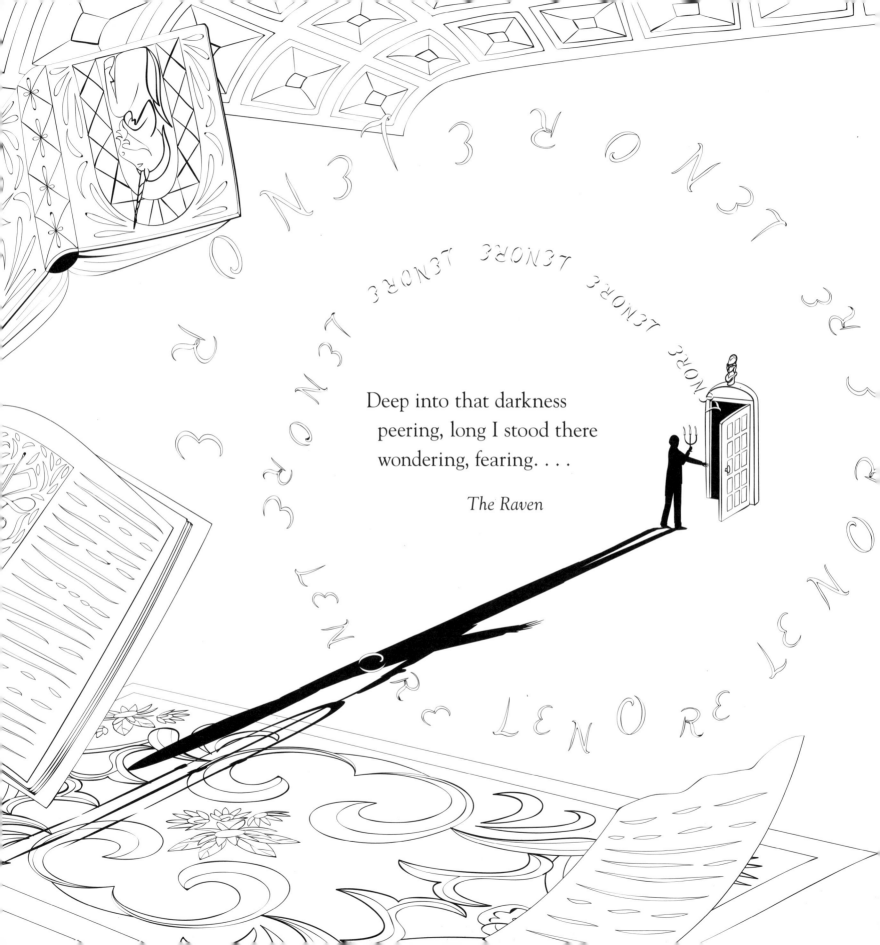

Deep into that darkness peering, long I stood there wondering, fearing. . . .

The Raven

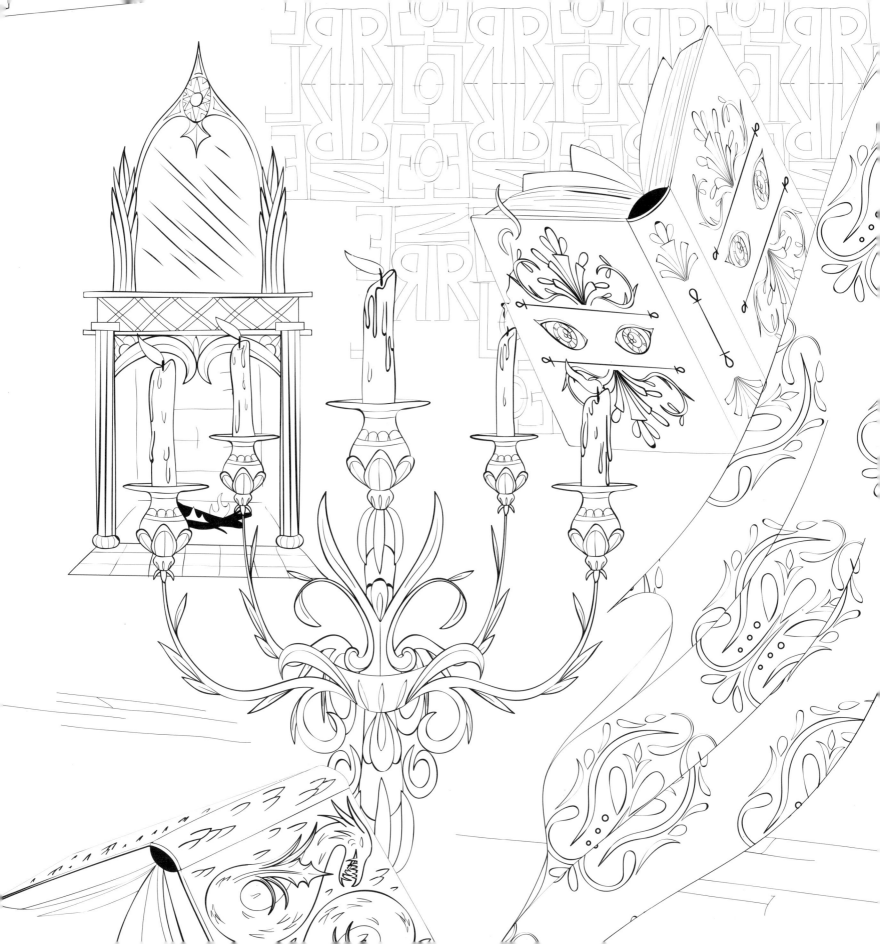

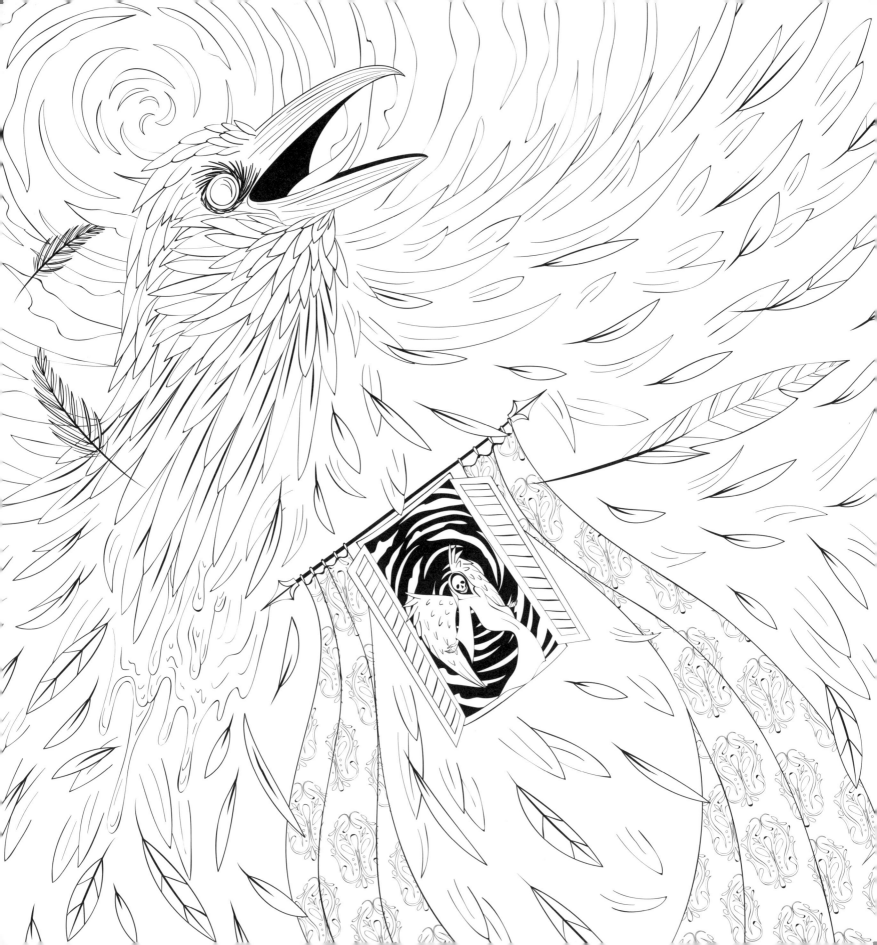

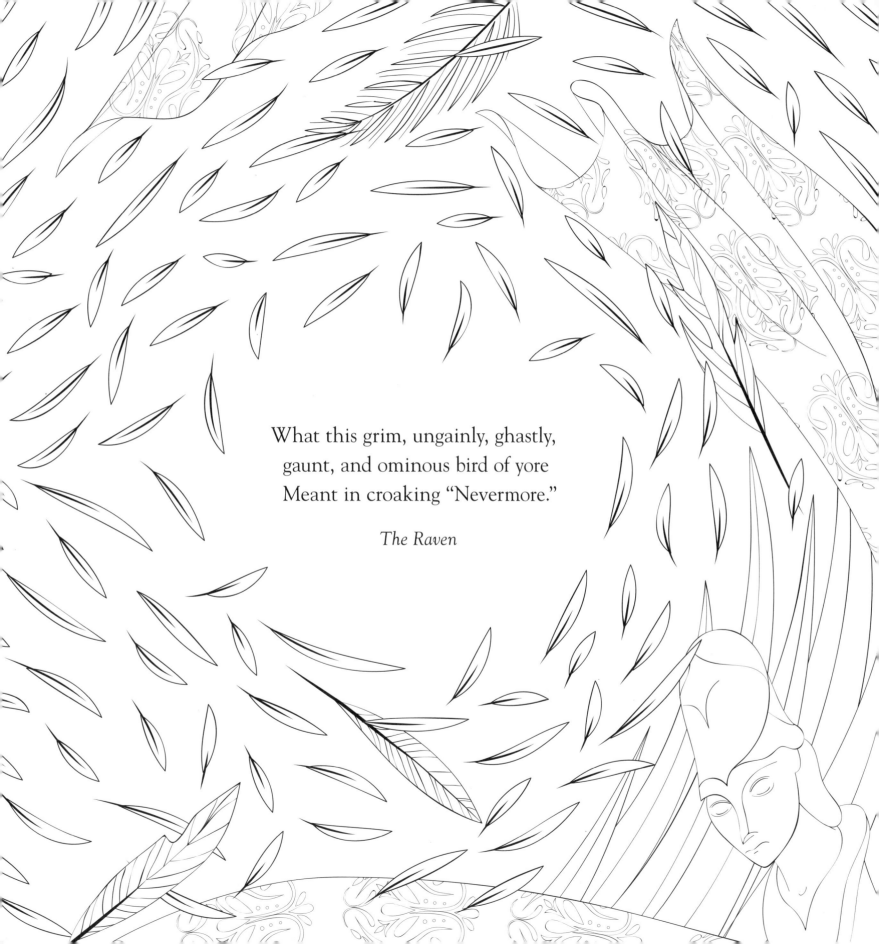

What this grim, ungainly, ghastly,
gaunt, and ominous bird of yore
Meant in croaking "Nevermore."

The Raven

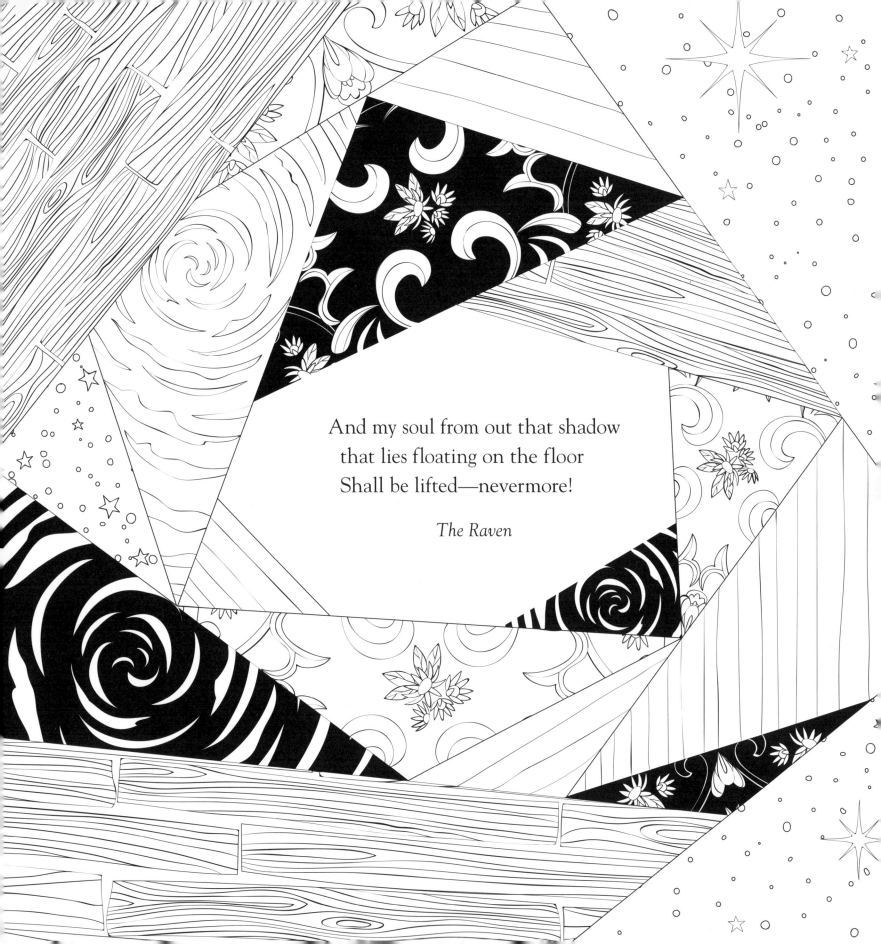

And my soul from out that shadow
that lies floating on the floor
Shall be lifted—nevermore!

The Raven

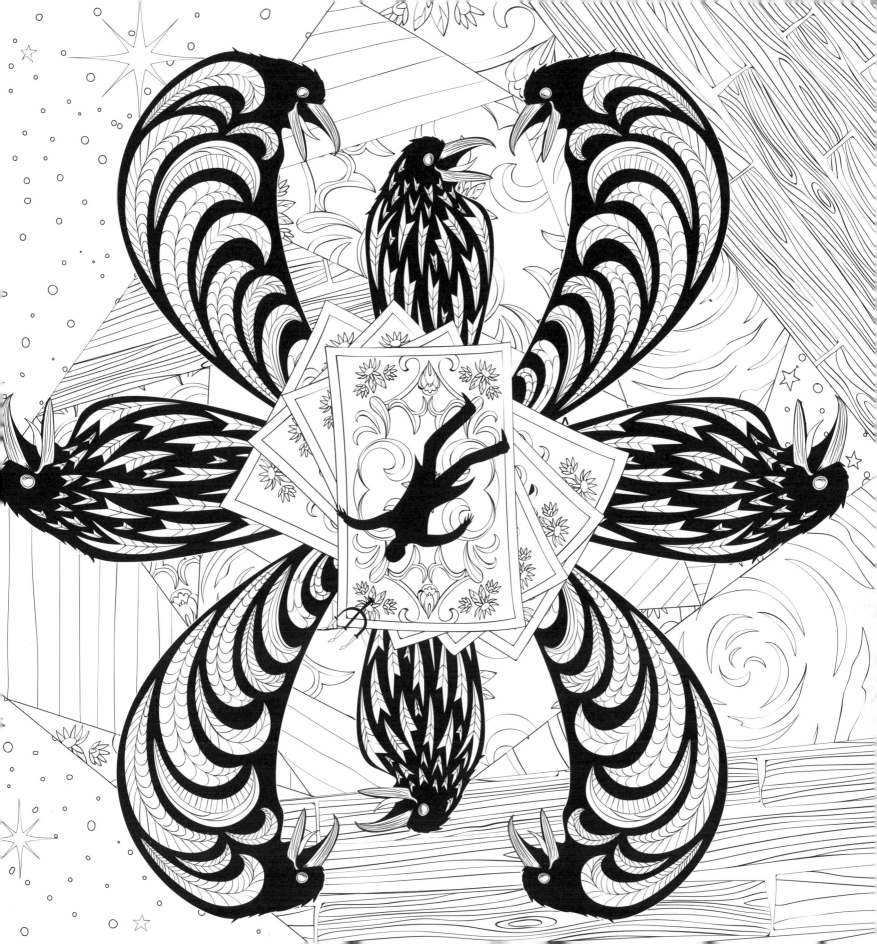

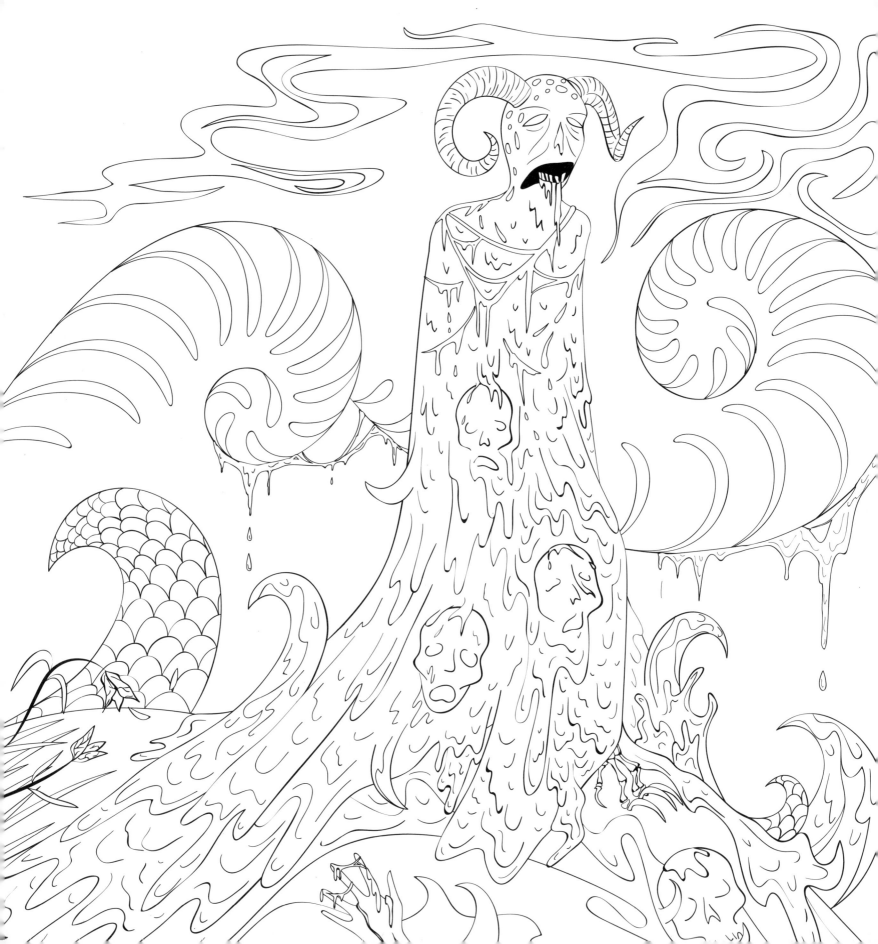

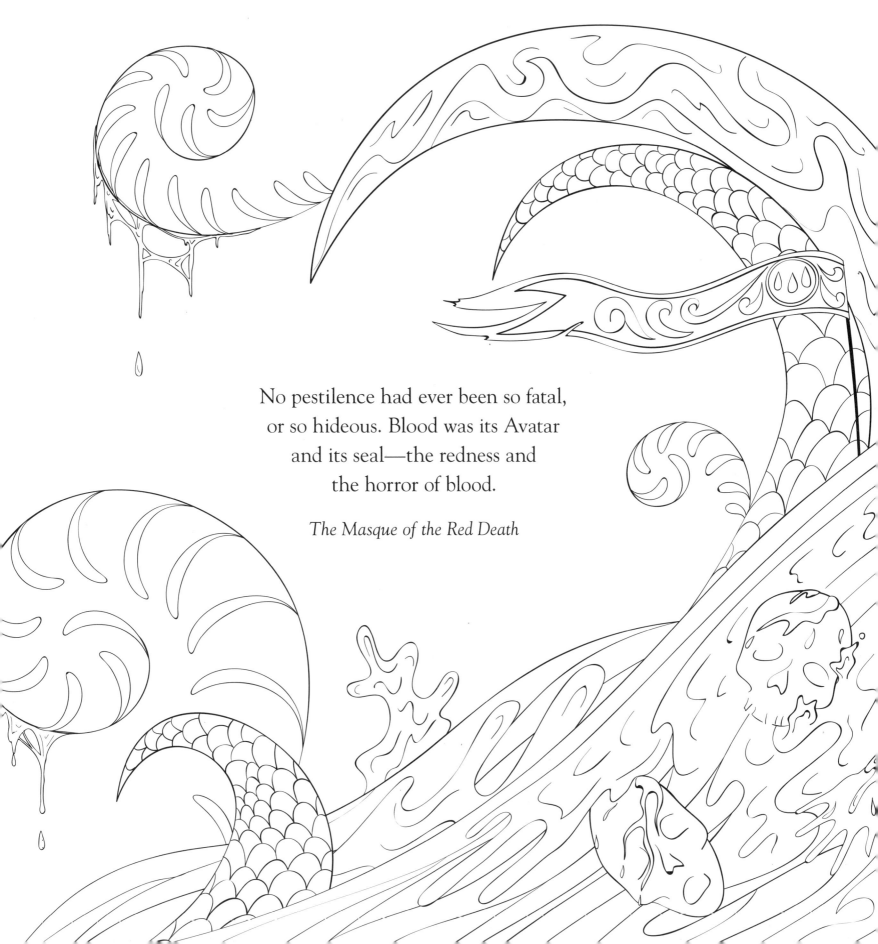

No pestilence had ever been so fatal,
or so hideous. Blood was its Avatar
and its seal—the redness and
the horror of blood.

The Masque of the Red Death

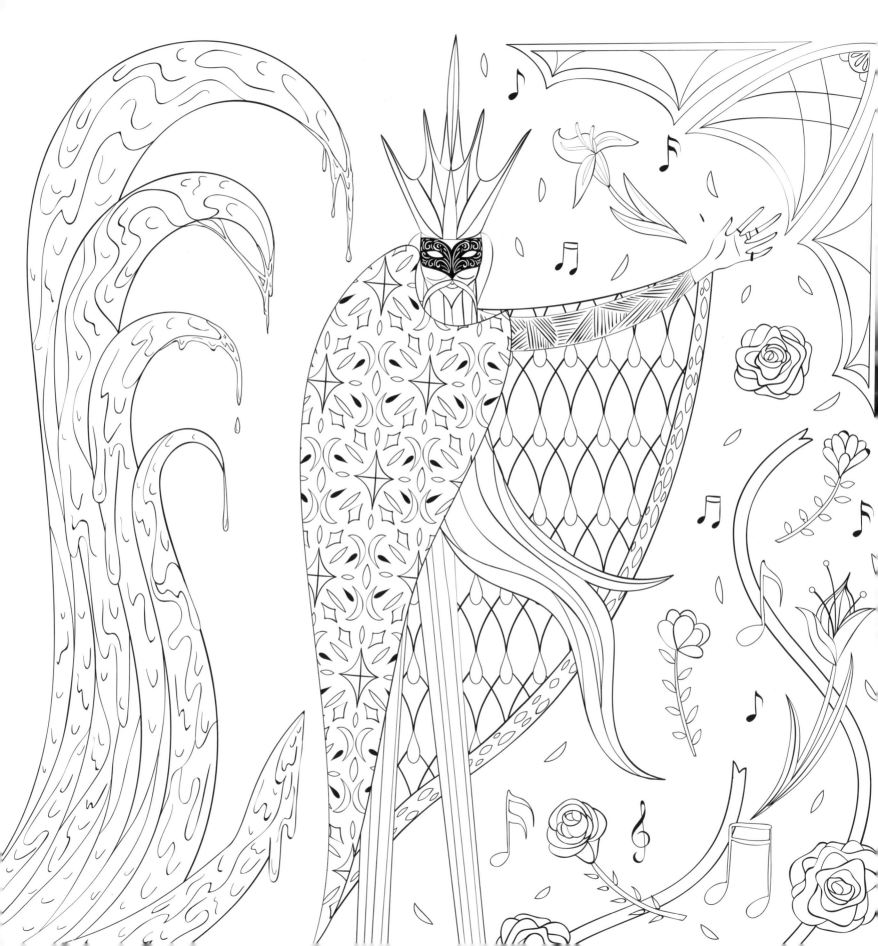

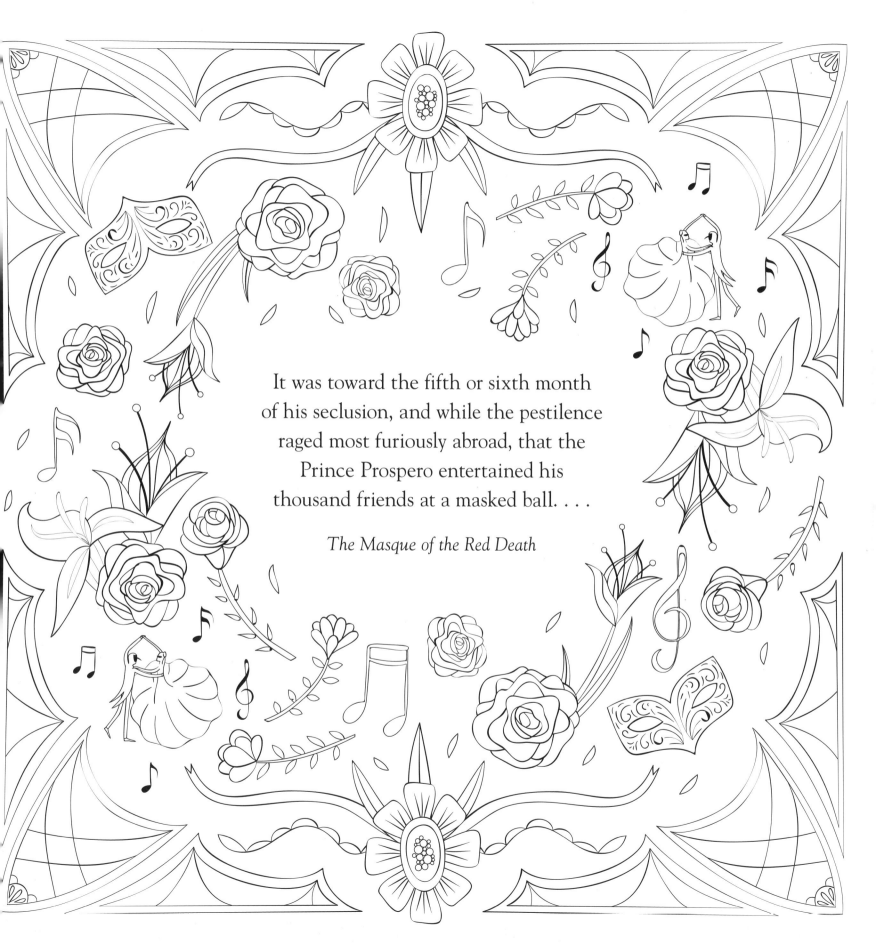

It was toward the fifth or sixth month of his seclusion, and while the pestilence raged most furiously abroad, that the Prince Prospero entertained his thousand friends at a masked ball. . . .

The Masque of the Red Death

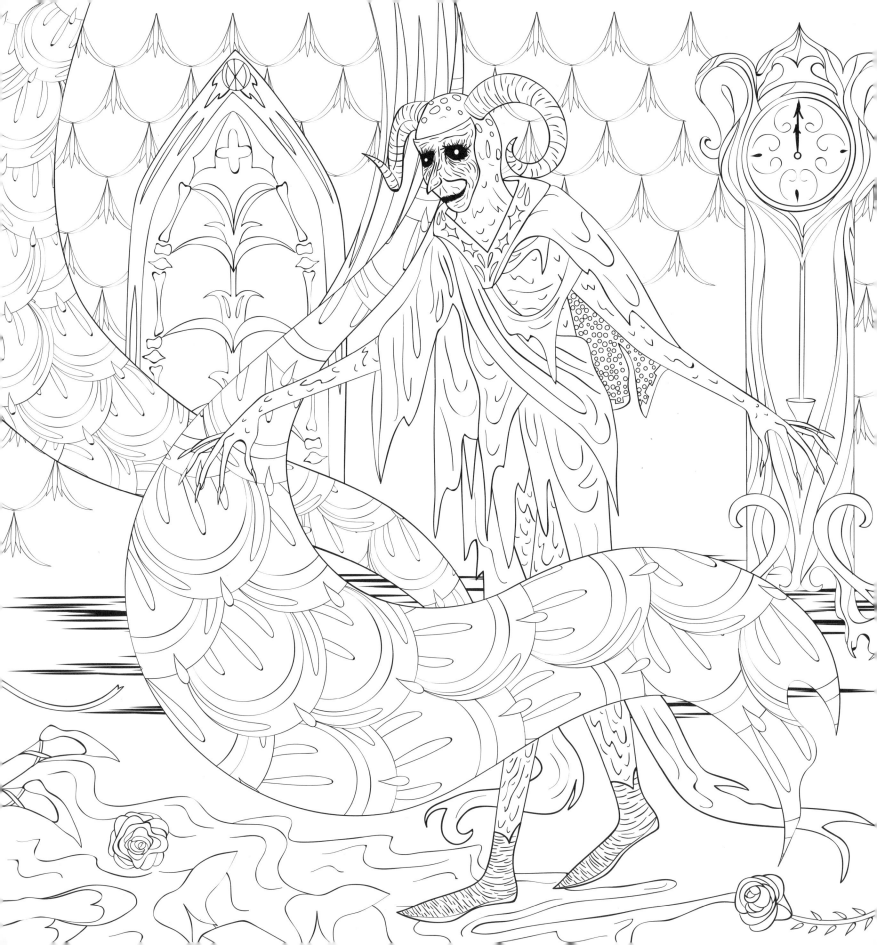

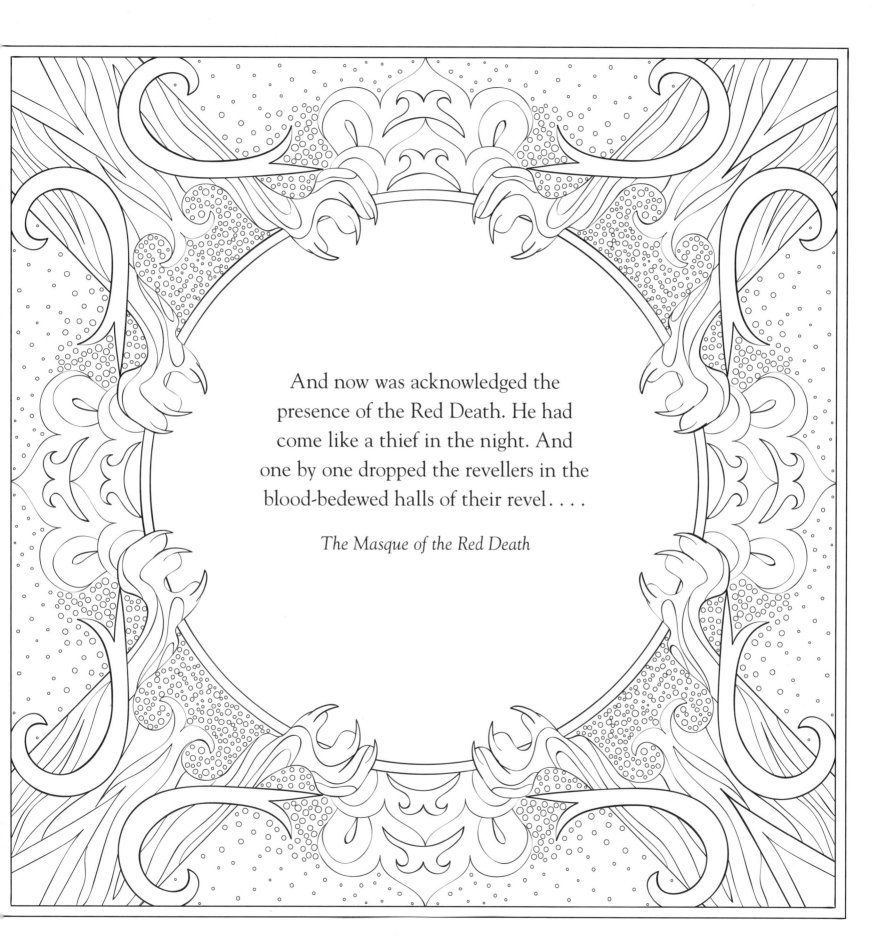

And now was acknowledged the presence of the Red Death. He had come like a thief in the night. And one by one dropped the revellers in the blood-bedewed halls of their revel. . . .

The Masque of the Red Death

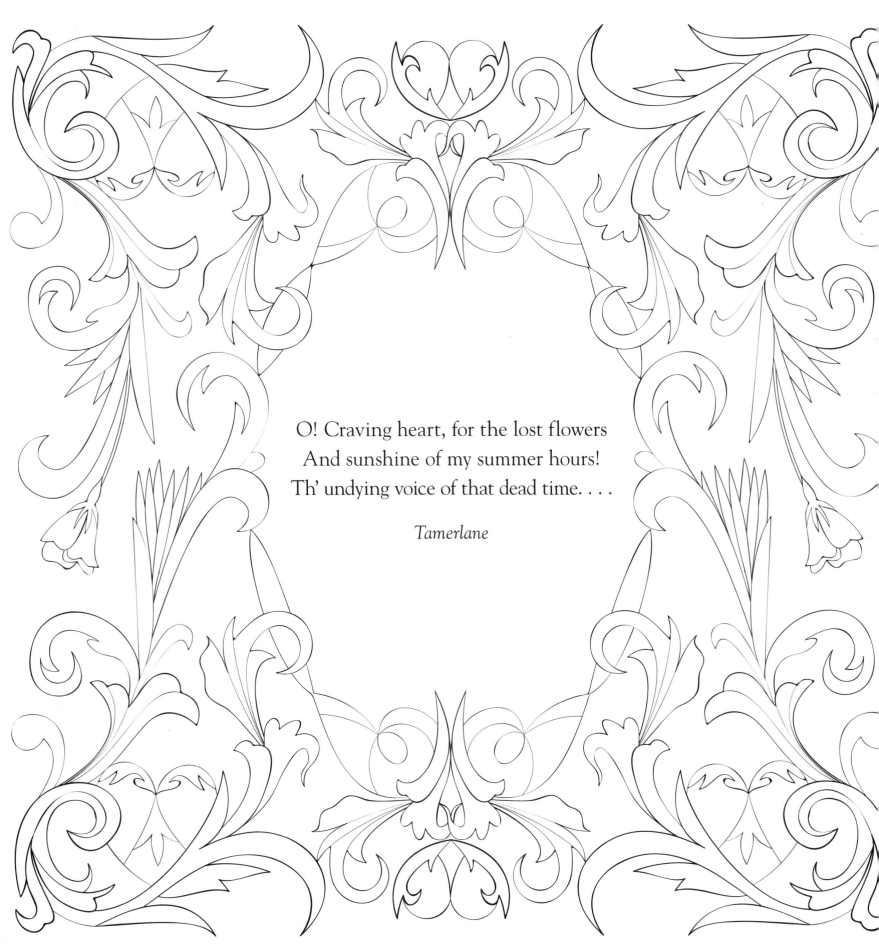

O! Craving heart, for the lost flowers
And sunshine of my summer hours!
Th' undying voice of that dead time. . . .

Tamerlane

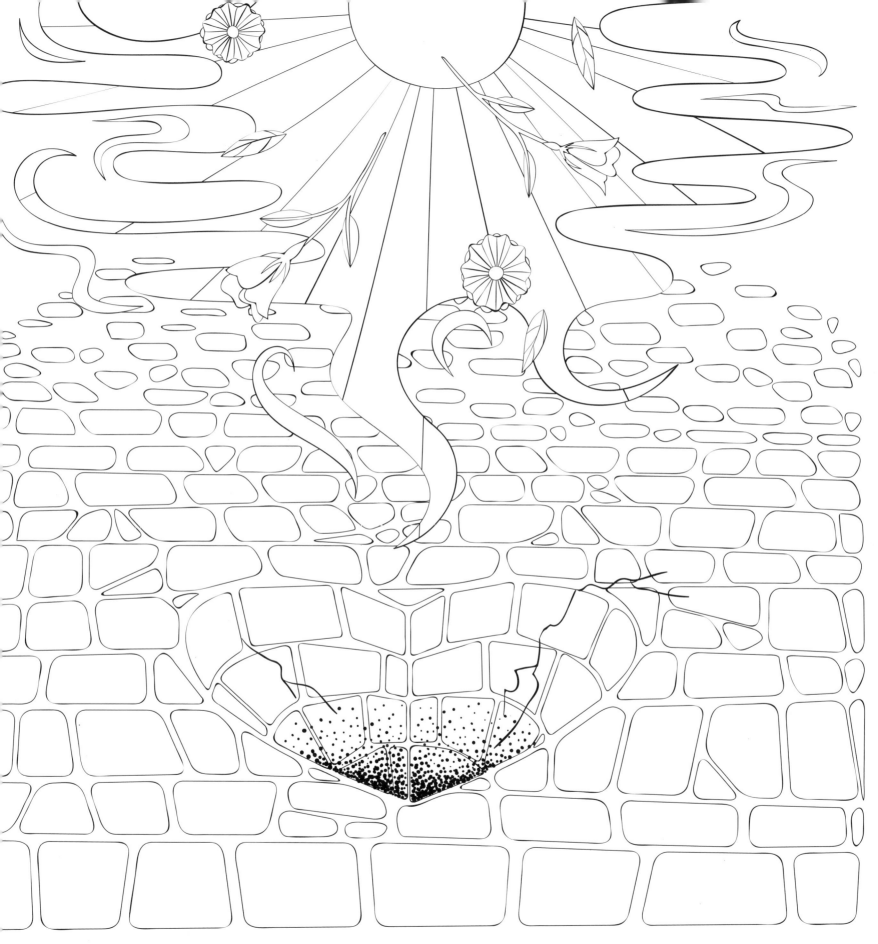

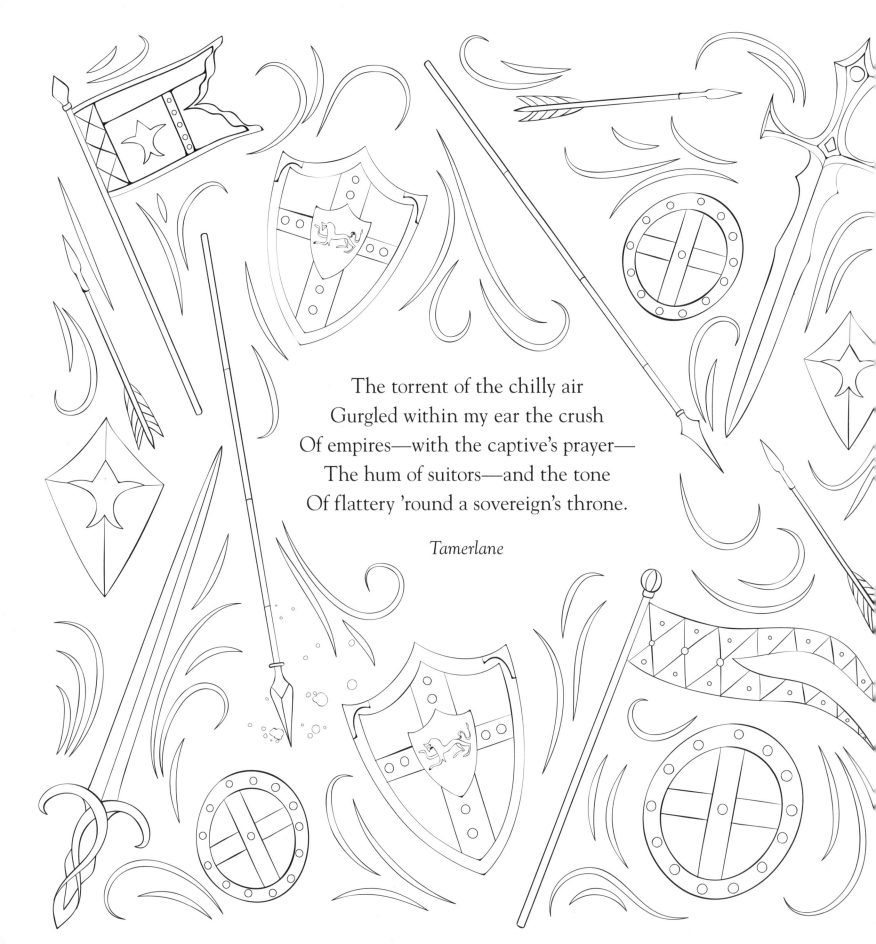

The torrent of the chilly air
Gurgled within my ear the crush
Of empires—with the captive's prayer—
The hum of suitors—and the tone
Of flattery 'round a sovereign's throne.

Tamerlane

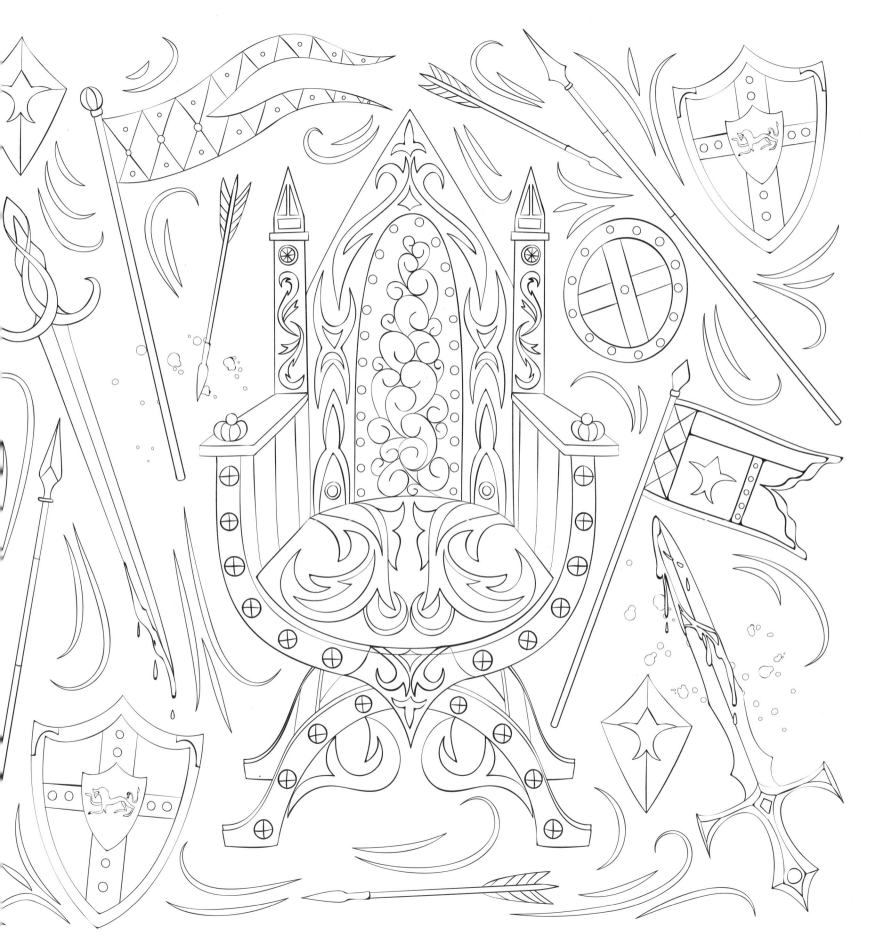

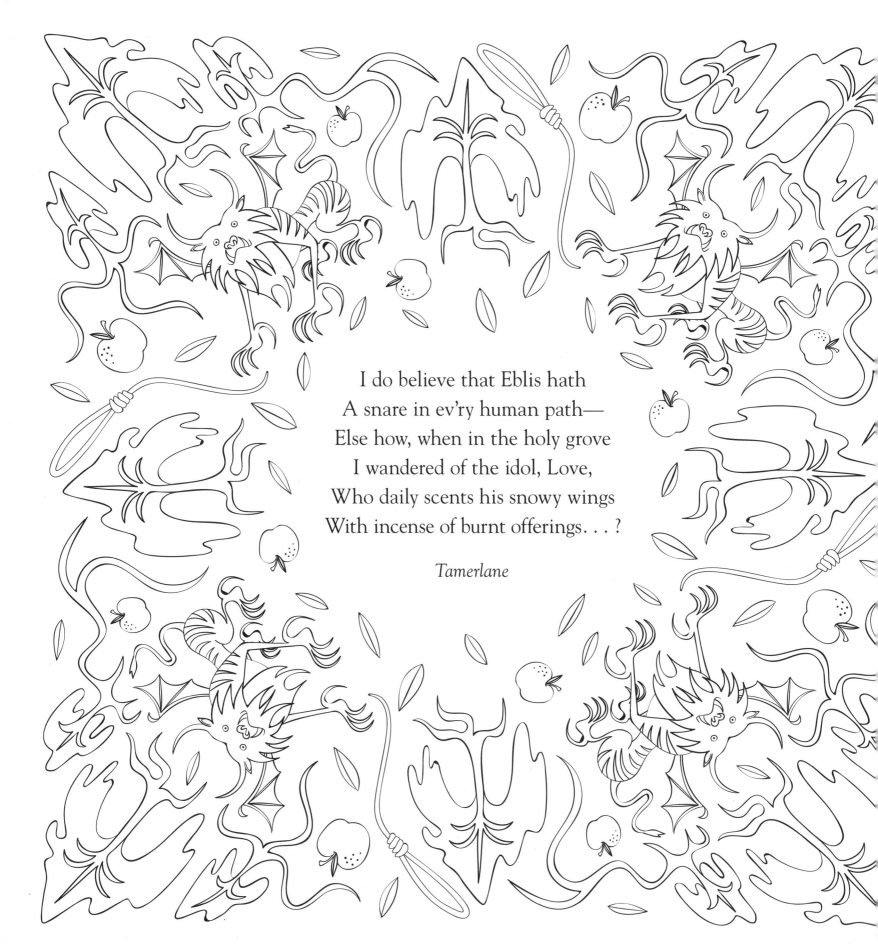

I do believe that Eblis hath
A snare in ev'ry human path—
Else how, when in the holy grove
I wandered of the idol, Love,
Who daily scents his snowy wings
With incense of burnt offerings. . . ?

Tamerlane

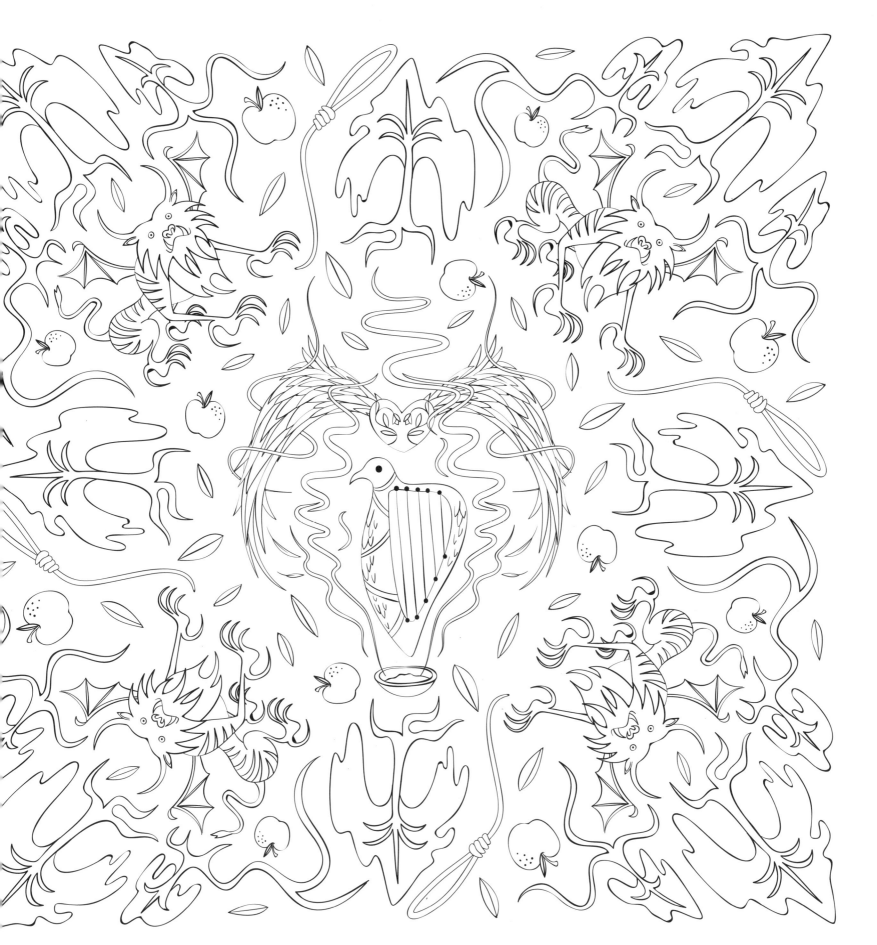

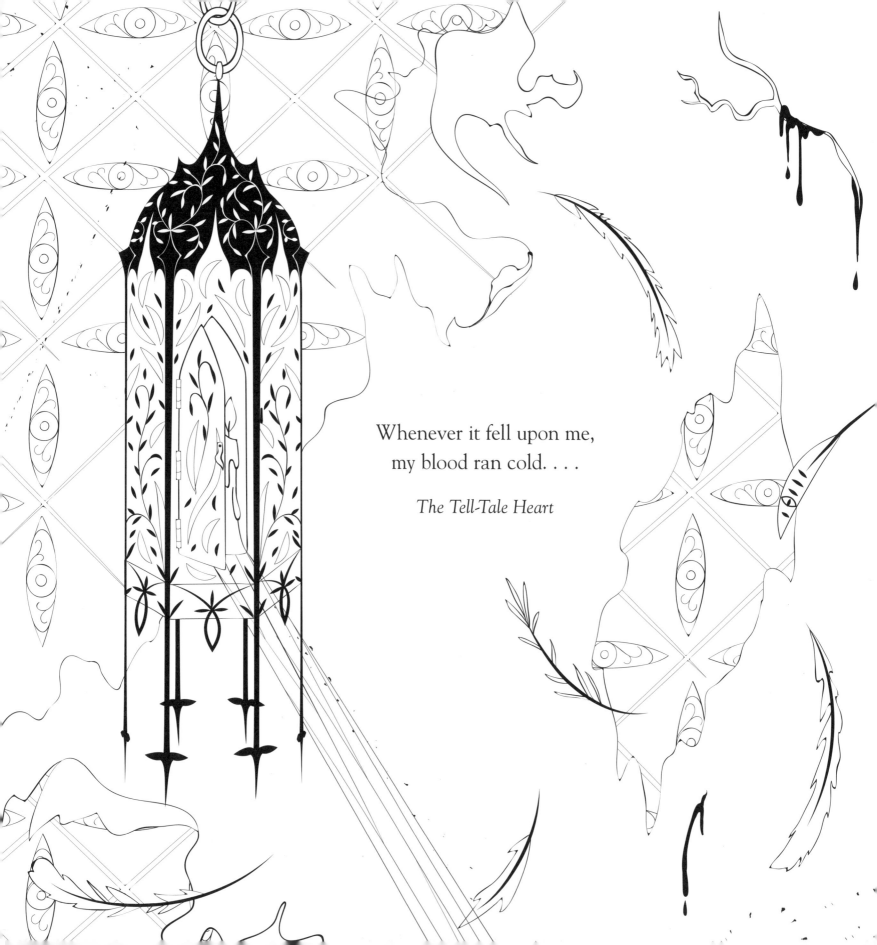

Whenever it fell upon me,
my blood ran cold. . . .

The Tell-Tale Heart

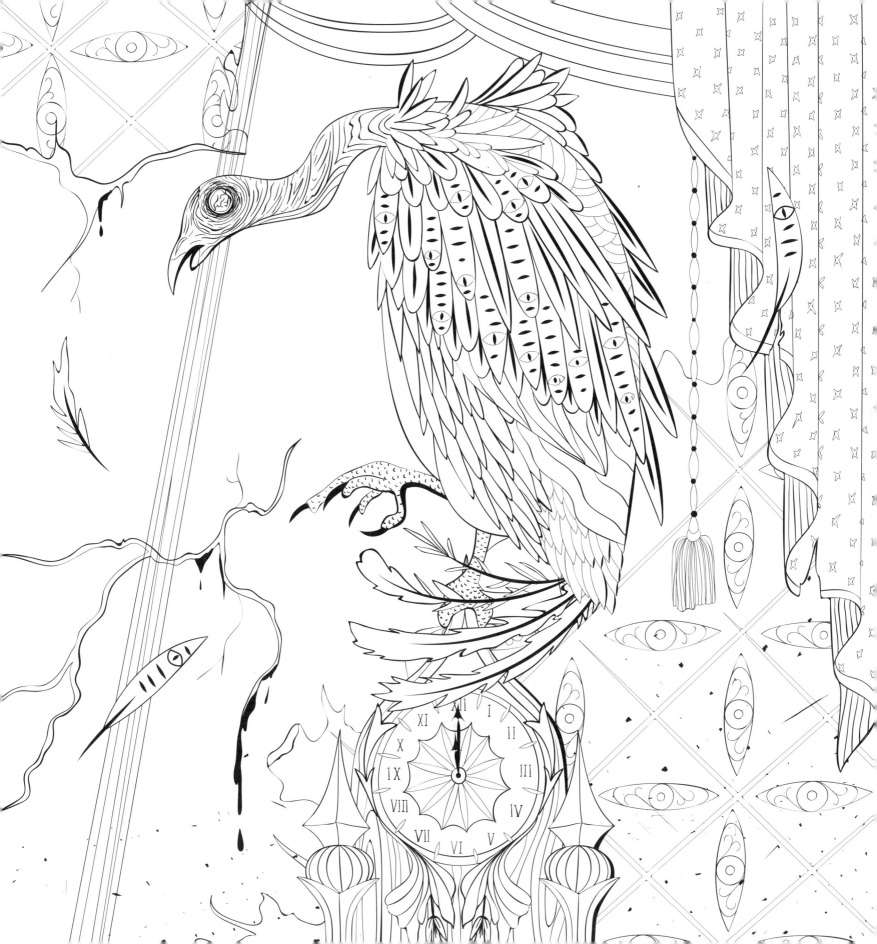

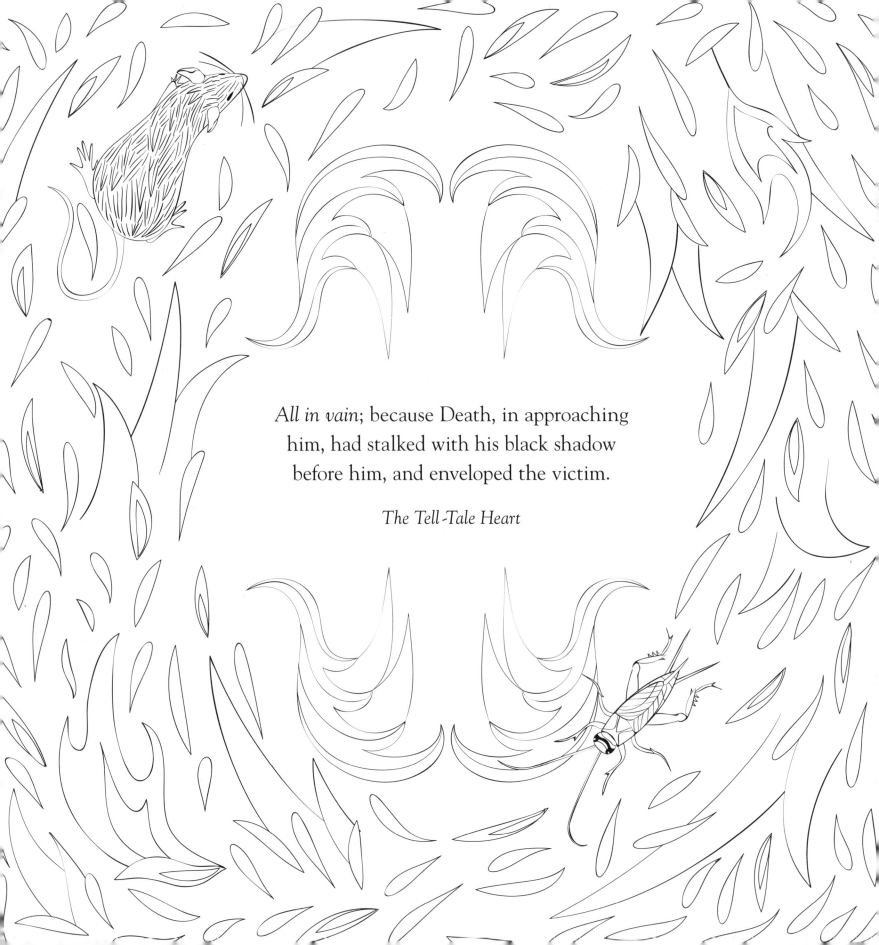

All in vain; because Death, in approaching him, had stalked with his black shadow before him, and enveloped the victim.

The Tell-Tale Heart

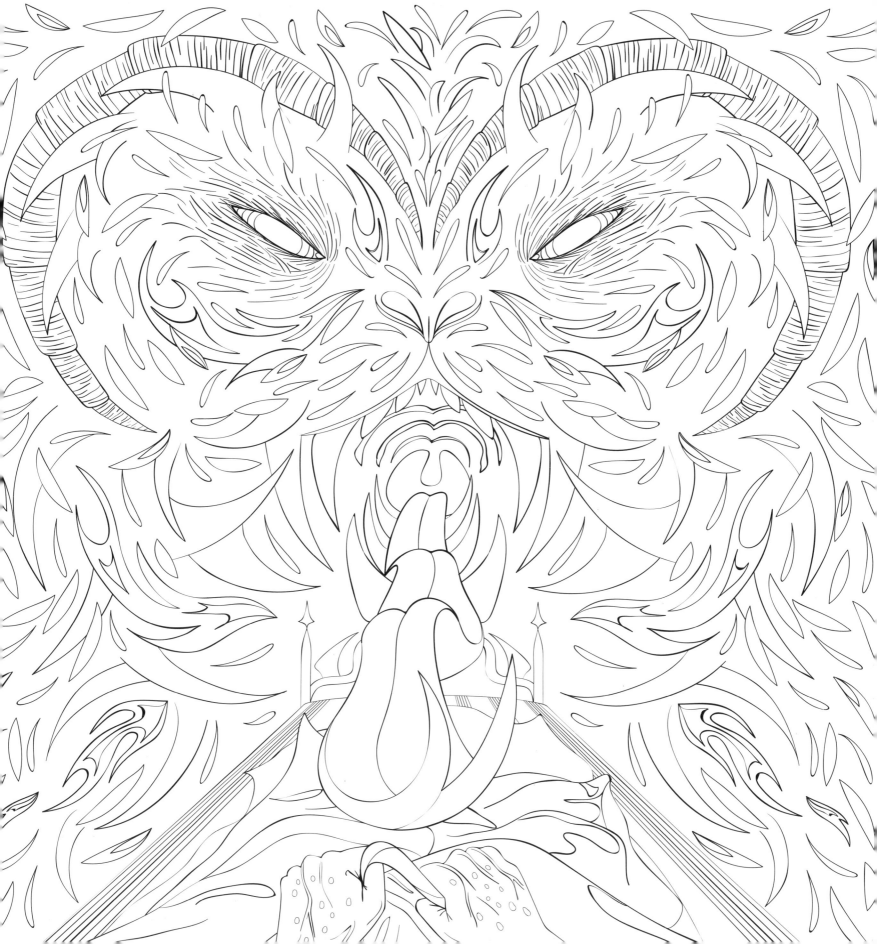

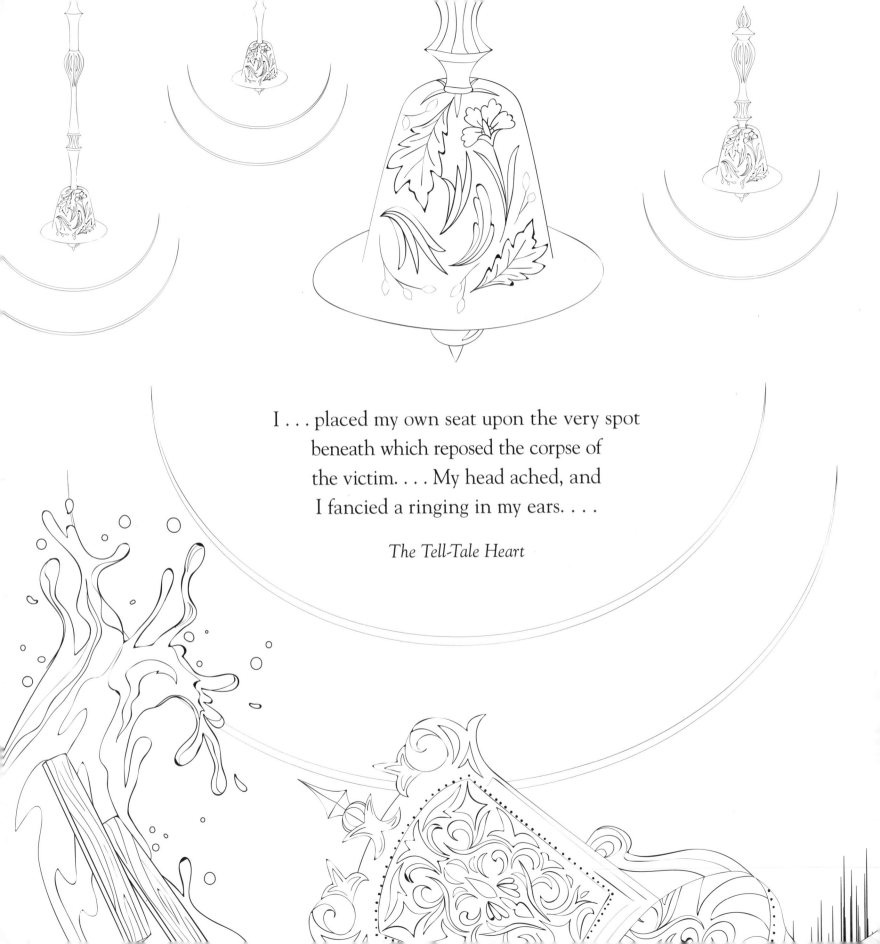

I . . . placed my own seat upon the very spot
beneath which reposed the corpse of
the victim. . . . My head ached, and
I fancied a ringing in my ears. . . .

The Tell-Tale Heart

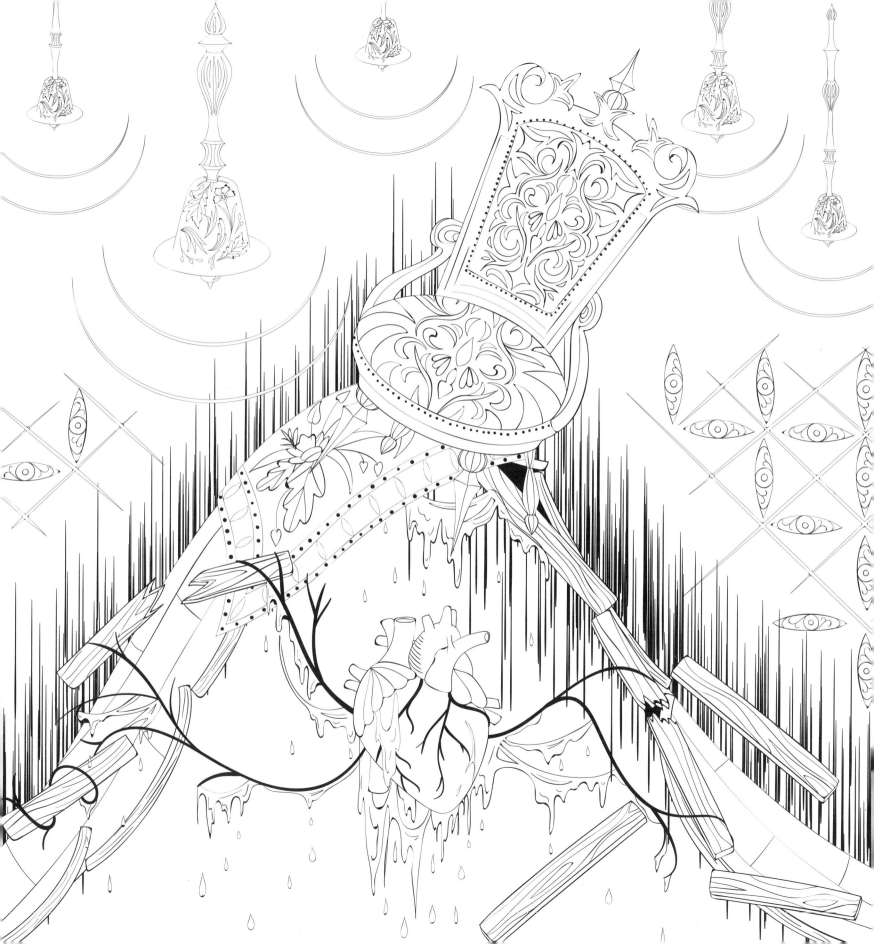

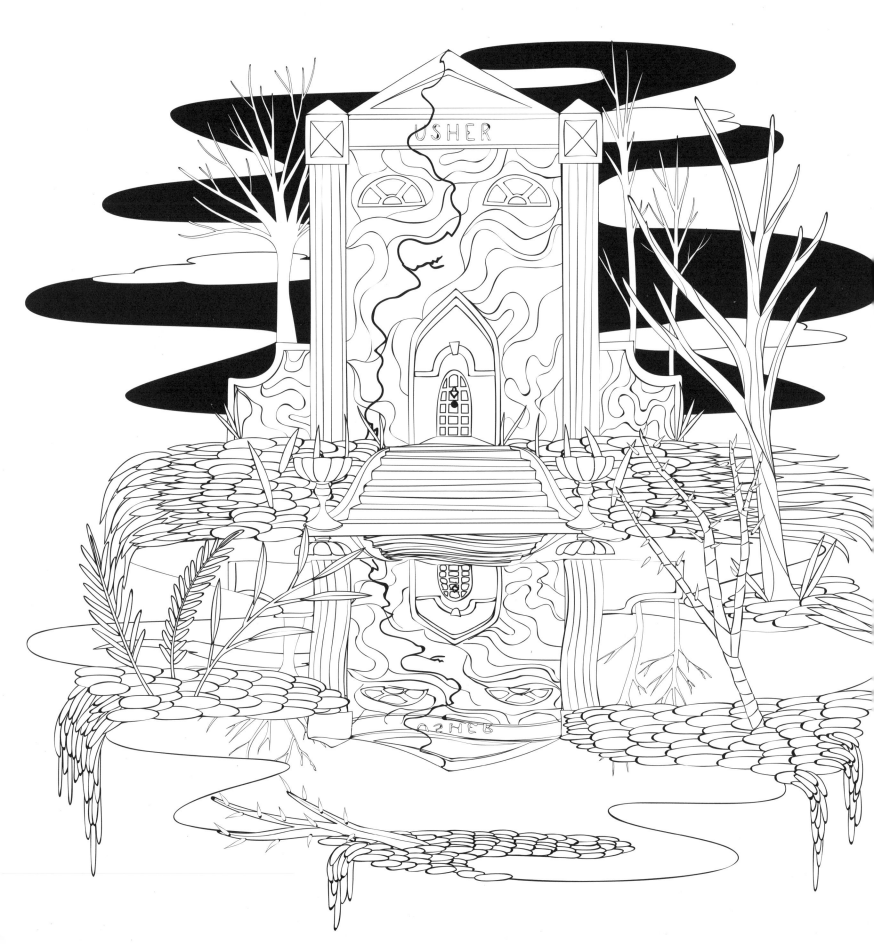

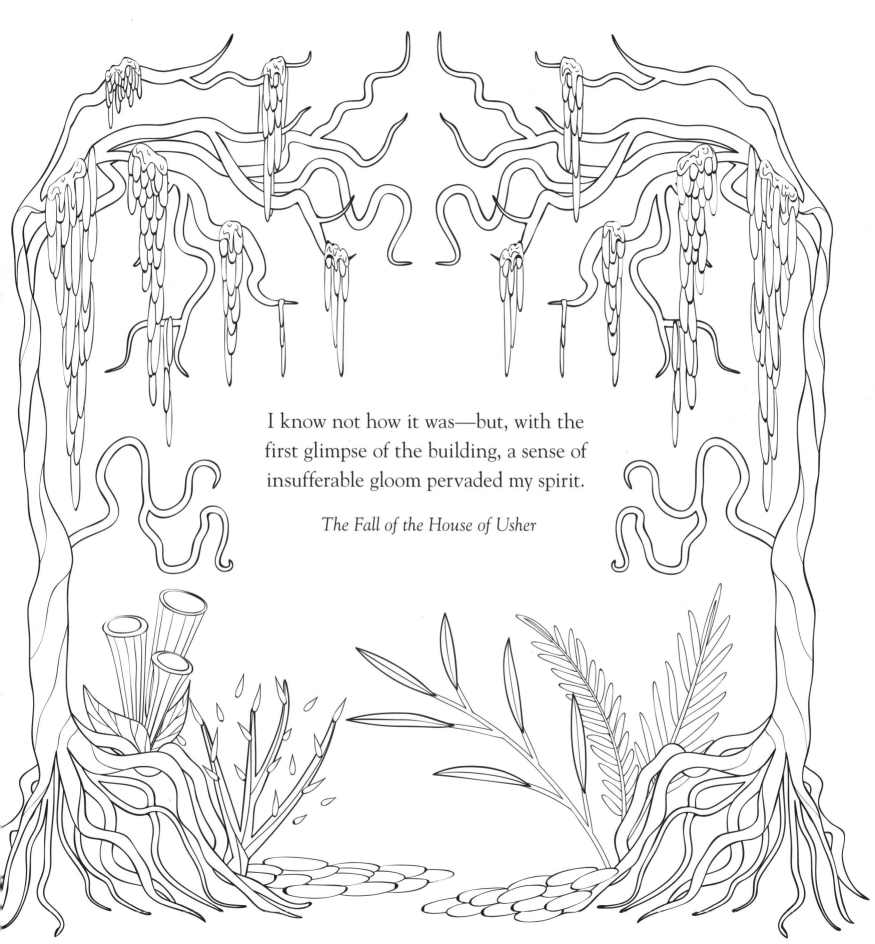

I know not how it was—but, with the
first glimpse of the building, a sense of
insufferable gloom pervaded my spirit.

The Fall of the House of Usher

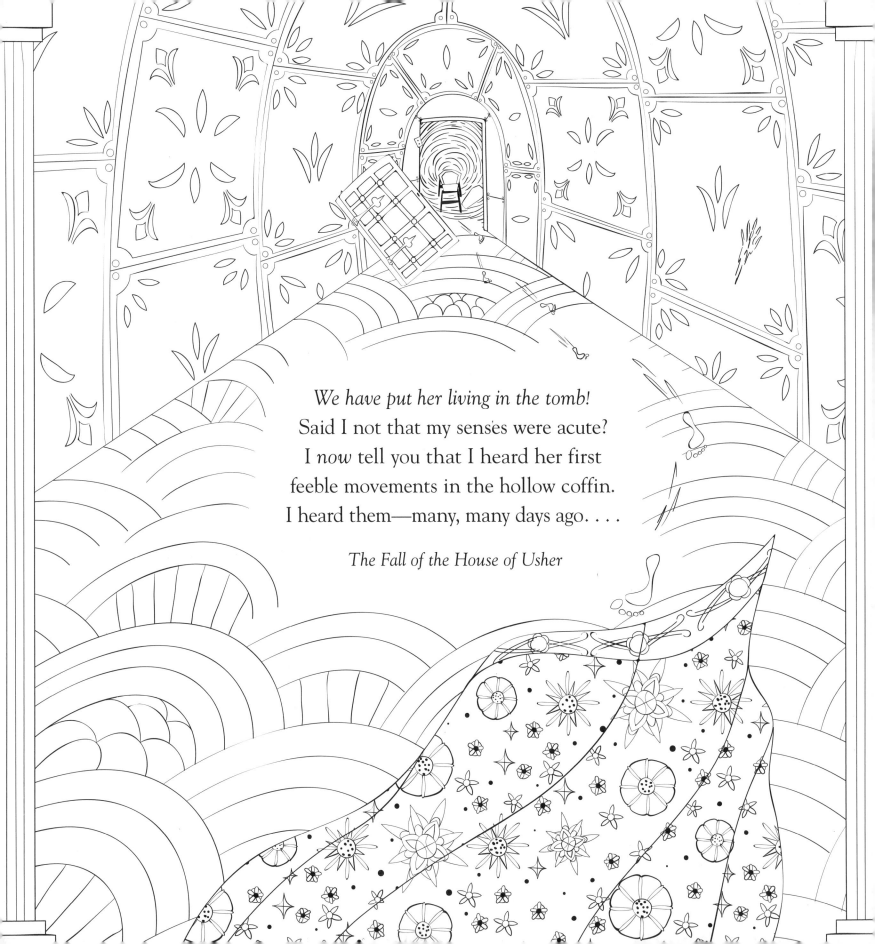

We have put her living in the tomb!
Said I not that my senses were acute?
I *now* tell you that I heard her first
feeble movements in the hollow coffin.
I heard them—many, many days ago. . . .

The Fall of the House of Usher

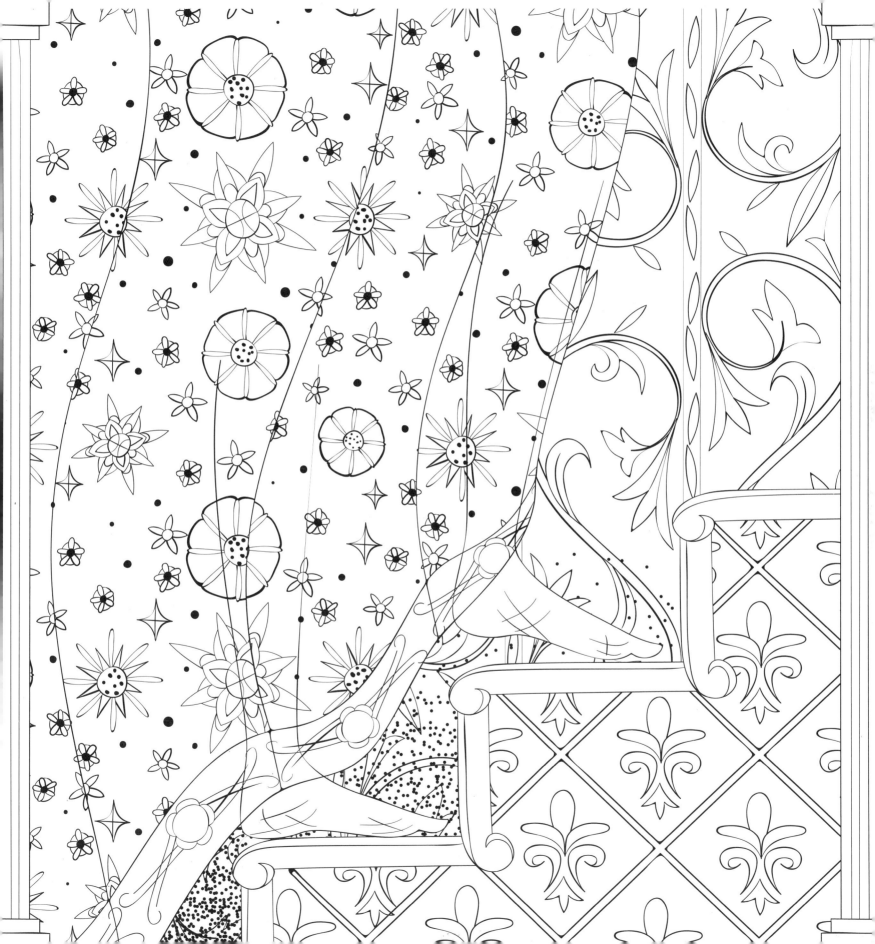

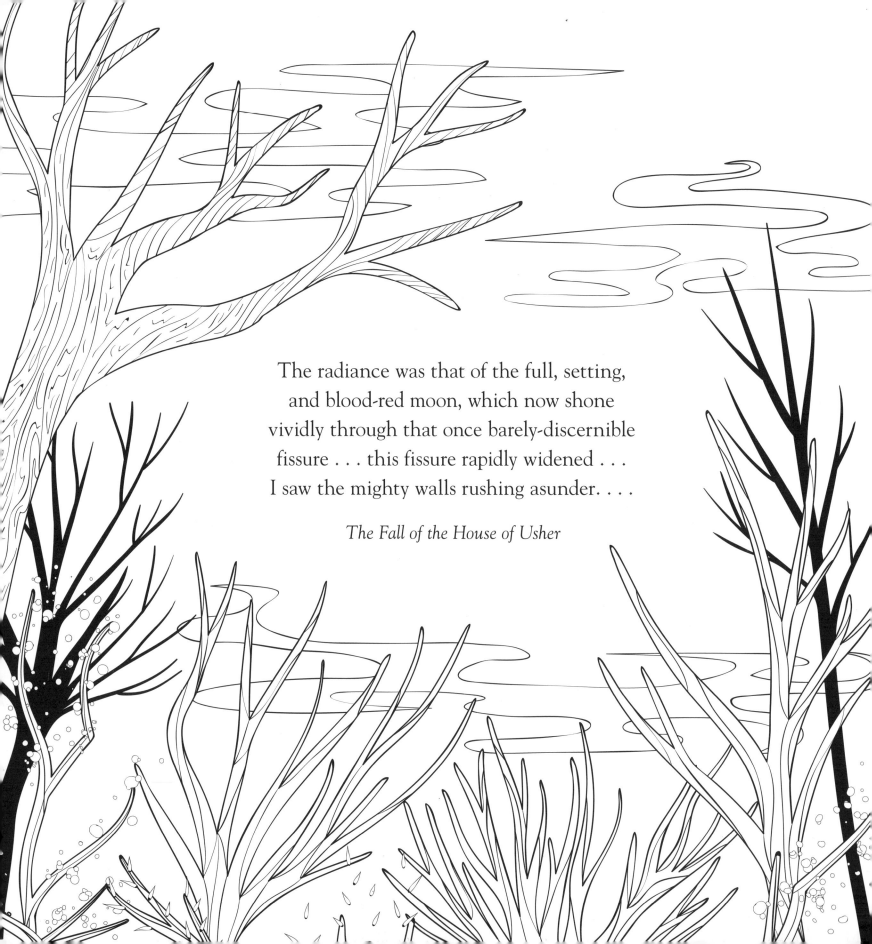

The radiance was that of the full, setting,
and blood-red moon, which now shone
vividly through that once barely-discernible
fissure . . . this fissure rapidly widened . . .
I saw the mighty walls rushing asunder. . . .

The Fall of the House of Usher

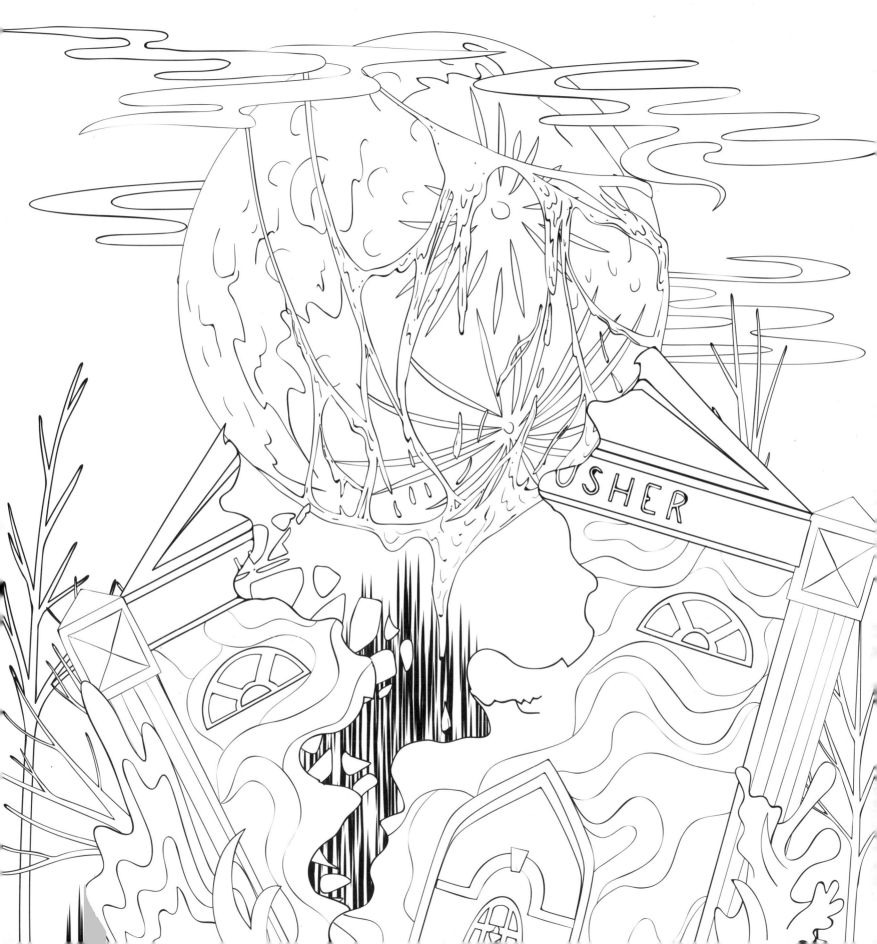

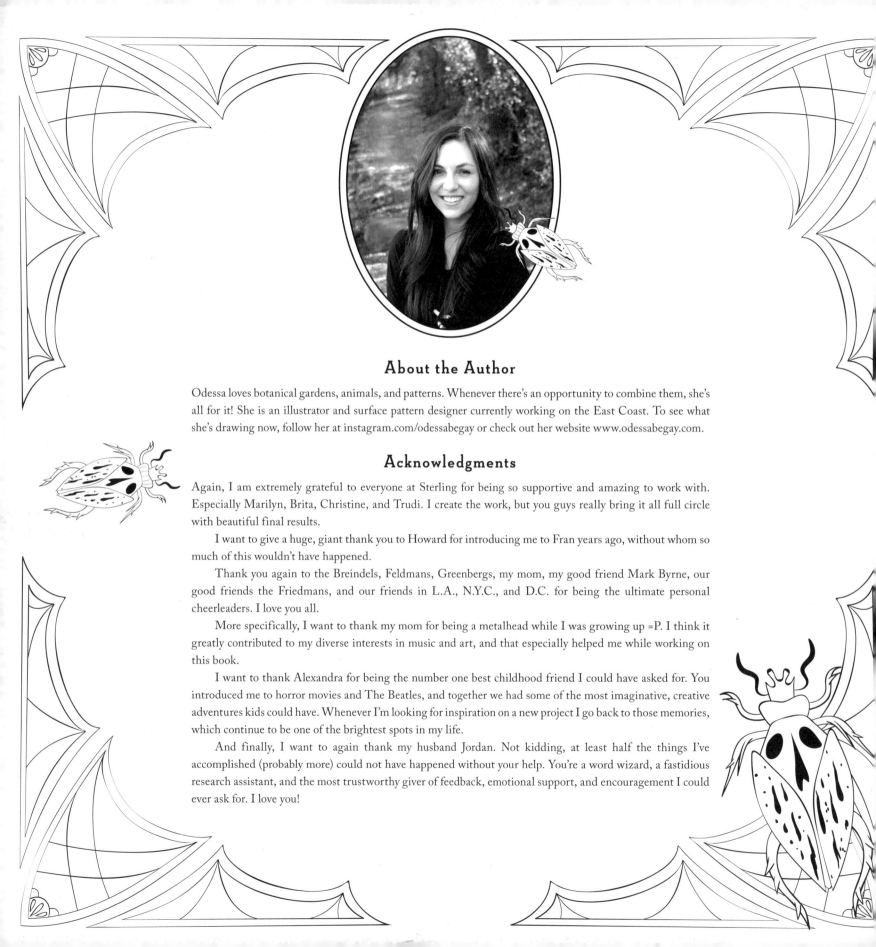

About the Author

Odessa loves botanical gardens, animals, and patterns. Whenever there's an opportunity to combine them, she's all for it! She is an illustrator and surface pattern designer currently working on the East Coast. To see what she's drawing now, follow her at instagram.com/odessabegay or check out her website www.odessabegay.com.

Acknowledgments

Again, I am extremely grateful to everyone at Sterling for being so supportive and amazing to work with. Especially Marilyn, Brita, Christine, and Trudi. I create the work, but you guys really bring it all full circle with beautiful final results.

I want to give a huge, giant thank you to Howard for introducing me to Fran years ago, without whom so much of this wouldn't have happened.

Thank you again to the Breindels, Feldmans, Greenbergs, my mom, my good friend Mark Byrne, our good friends the Friedmans, and our friends in L.A., N.Y.C., and D.C. for being the ultimate personal cheerleaders. I love you all.

More specifically, I want to thank my mom for being a metalhead while I was growing up =P. I think it greatly contributed to my diverse interests in music and art, and that especially helped me while working on this book.

I want to thank Alexandra for being the number one best childhood friend I could have asked for. You introduced me to horror movies and The Beatles, and together we had some of the most imaginative, creative adventures kids could have. Whenever I'm looking for inspiration on a new project I go back to those memories, which continue to be one of the brightest spots in my life.

And finally, I want to again thank my husband Jordan. Not kidding, at least half the things I've accomplished (probably more) could not have happened without your help. You're a word wizard, a fastidious research assistant, and the most trustworthy giver of feedback, emotional support, and encouragement I could ever ask for. I love you!